A Tiger's Walk

Memoirs of an Auburn Football Player

To Harry
Happy Birthday: Best Wishes !

Rob Pate

Rob 31
Pate

Sports Publishing L.L.C.
www.sportspublishingllc.com

Director of production: Susan M. Moyer
Project manager: Jim Henehan
Dust jacket design: Christine Mohrbacher
Developmental editor: Elisa Bock Laird
Copy editor: Cynthia L. McNew
Photo editor: Erin Linden-Levy
Imaging: Kerri Baker, Christine Mohrbacher

ISBN: 1-58261-311-7

Printed in the United States of America.

Sports Publishing L.L.C.
www.sportspublishingllc.com

To my wife, Dana, who has supported me and taught me how to love; to my daughter, Claire McKinley, who is the light of my life; to my parents, Mike and Darlene, who never missed a single game I played in; to my brothers, David and Phillip, who taught me how to be tough; to the late Brian Tribble, whose life was truly inspirational; to Tim Cole, who taught me the game of football; to Bill Oliver, whom I love like a father; to Justin McBurney, who showed me the meaning of Auburn football; to the late Jim Fyffe, who embodied the very definition of the Auburn Spirit; and to all my teammates who can relate to my story, to you this book is dedicated.

CONTENTS

FOREWORD

"**R**aw D on 3! 1…2…3…RAW—D!" When I heard Rob Pate shout these words, I knew then it was game time. The quietness of the room during pregame meals let me know something special was in the near future. The bus ride to the game where the conglomeration of everything from Master P and R. Kelly to Guns 'n' Roses and Hank Williams Jr. made me aware of a festive atmosphere. Walking down Tiger Walk where family, friends, and maniac fans encouraged their favorite soldiers energized me for the war that lay ahead. Walking around the field visualizing making highlight plays narrowed the focus of my mind to a single objective. Warmups got the blood flowing, and the screams from the crowd got the heart racing. But it wasn't game time until Rob Pate spoke.

And he's about to speak again.

I hope you are ready for the journey you're about to take and the places you're about to go, because you are going to hear and see things that you've never heard or seen before. Forget about all of the fairy tales you've read in the newspaper or seen on ESPN. This book wasn't written by some reporter who played flag football with his fraternity brothers, a lifelong Auburn fan who has never missed a game, or some PlayStation warrior who never had the balls to put on a helmet. Rob Pate has been, is, and always will be a winner, and this book is a winner as well. And when the clock finally runs out and you've read his story, I know you also will feel like a winner. You are about to put on the helmet of No. 31 and see through his eyes the four years he spent on the Plains.

However, Rob's story is like every college football player's story—the position or school doesn't matter. So if you've ever wondered what really goes on after the cameras are shut off, the fans leave, and the lights go out, get ready. The pages ahead reveal the real life of a college athlete today. There is no sugar coating, and there are no sweet words to make everybody happy. Just the truth.

I lived with Rob our first two years at Auburn, and I, along with everyone who has ever met him, know him as a lot of things, but never a fake. And neither is his story. Reading the pages ahead is going to be like going through a game yourself. It's going to be a roller-coaster ride through emotions, injuries, and relationships, and in the end you're going to know the real deal. You're going to know what college football is all about. From the inside out.

I love Rob Pate. I love who he is. I love what he stands for. I'll be the luckiest father in the world if one day just one of my children turns out like him. I can hear him now just as I did our freshman year in Sewell Hall. He's lying in the bunk bed above mine telling me to quit talking. It's almost game time.

He's got something to say. I hope you're ready.

Whit Smith
Teammate and roommate
Auburn DE No. 42
1997–2000

ACKNOWLEDGMENTS

This book was made possible through the help and hard work of numerous people who wanted to see this story told even more so than myself in some instances. Thanks are due to all who provided chapter introductions: Tim Cole, Hal Riddle, Alex Lincoln, Phillip Lolley, and Phillip Pate. Thanks to Whit Smith for the superb foreword he contributed and to Ben Leard for the sincere afterword.

I owe deep gratitude to Paul Finebaum and the Finebaum Radio Network for allowing me to discuss the book on his immensely popular and widely heard radio program. This interview sparked the interest that resulted in the publishing of this book. Also to Charles Wright, an exceptional friend of mine who physically drove my manuscript to the Finebaum Radio Network, an action that prompted the interview and allowed me the media exposure needed to raise attention to my story.

Thanks are in order to Chip Mercer of BookLink, Inc. in Birmingham, Alabama, who listened to my interview on the Finebaum Network, read my manuscript, and put me in contact with Sports Publishing L.L.C.

Thanks to Scott Musgrave, an acquisitions editor at Sports Publishing who walked me through all of the intricacies of the book business and contract procedures, items I was an absolute novice on.

Thanks to Elisa Bock Laird, a developmental editor at Sports Publishing for keeping me straight on due dates, how things were developing, and just being a professional and easy to work with. Her hard work and many suggestions added significantly to this book, and her proficiency was remarkable.

Thanks go out to Phillip Marshall and Mark Murphy for providing excerpts from my book on the "Inside the Auburn Tigers" web site. Also to Bill Cameron and Andy Burcham for allowing me time on their local radio call-in show in the Auburn-Opelika area, station 1230AM WAUD.

To Meredith Jenkins and Kirk Sampson of the Auburn Media Relations Department for providing me with the vast majority of the pictures featured in this book, as well as being two of the finest representatives Auburn could hope to have.

Thanks to all of my family, immediate and extended, and friends for reading and listening to my work in progress at all of the various stages and for encouraging me to finish what I had started.

I especially need to thank my dad, Mike Pate, for his advice and willingness to listen to my work. He was the editor before the editor.

Special thanks to my wife for allowing me to pursue this endeavor unopposed and without guilt for the time it took me away from my family. What an extraordinary partner I have in Dana.

Finally, as a believer in Christ Jesus, to Him I give all glory, honor, and praise for allowing this book to reach its completion. I am a man of devout Christian faith, and I hope that as you read this sentence, you know, for sure, where your eternity lies. As the saying goes, "He who provides for this life, but does not take care for eternity is wise for a moment, but a fool forever."

INTRODUCTION

I guess I've always known that college football was the livelihood of this state. I think everyone who grows up in the state of Alabama knows and appreciates the tradition and pageantry that comes with football, in particular college football at Auburn University and the University of Alabama. Since I was five, football has been a way of life for me. In this state, the ultimate goal and dream of just about every little boy is to wear the orange and blue of Auburn or the crimson and white of Alabama. For four years I lived that dream as an Auburn Tiger. I was a four-year defensive starter who played at Auburn in the midst of a tremendous storm of controversy as well as unparalleled success. I played on two teams that represented the western side of the conference in Atlanta as champions, and I played on two teams that had miserable losing seasons. I played for Coach Terry Bowden, who holds the record at Auburn for the best winning percentage of all time, and I played for Coach Tommy Tuberville, who is one of the most sought after and respected coaches in all of the land. And through all of this, I have been taking notes—mental notes that are fresh in my memory as well as actual notes in my senior year journal. I want to share with you what this obsession is all about. I want people to see the truth, both good and bad, for what it's worth. I'll take you on an incredible journey from a little park in my hometown to the bright lights of Auburn football. I want you to take a trip with me, No. 31, Rob Pate, so that I can introduce you to college football in the new millennium.

CHAPTER 1

Ready or Not, Here I Come

Born to play.

I had the privilege of coaching Rob Pate for five consecutive years beginning in 1985. I nicknamed him "Chubby" the very first year, not because he was overweight, but because he was always starving himself to be under the weight limit just so he could participate—and participate he did.

He was a delightful youngster with great desire, not to mention the fact that he was the most talented child I had ever seen. Everything I wanted the kids to achieve as a team, we did. We posted five consecutive Alabama Youth Football State Championships, and Rob Pate was the driver. He pushed himself so hard that others followed. My job was easy. He led our team not only statistically, but also as a person. He never boasted, and he could have. He scored 72 touchdowns in a single season. He never was disrespectful, always the "awe-shucks" kind of kid, pointing to his teammates or his coaches. If he enjoyed the attention and spotlight, I never saw him show it.

In an era of taunting, trash talking, and showboating, which was frustrating for an old-fashioned coach, Rob always demonstrated class. I remember talking to him about keeping success in perspective, challenging him to drive to make his parents proud not only of his playing abilities, but also of his off-the-field attitude. I remember telling him it would pay great dividends one day.

To this day, he is the finest athlete that I personally have coached or known. I'm proud of that. I'm most proud of the man he has become.

Many thanks to Mike and Darlene for allowing a young coach to teach the perfect football student. I will always cherish the memories.

Tim Cole
Little League Football Coach
1985–1990

Football started out as a fun way to pass the time. What began in my front yard developed into a passion by the time I was in elementary school. Here I am with the Center Point Stallions at age five. *Courtesy of the author.*

Growing up in the small Birmingham suburb of Center Point, sports was about the only thing my brothers and I had to do. During the fall, we would play yard football. In the winter, basketball was the new thing. And in the spring, wiffle ball was the neighborhood substitute for baseball. And even though all three of us played park football and baseball, as well as church basketball at different age levels, the real games were held between the three of us on the streets of Center Point. That's where the competitive drive and determination to be the absolute best first took root in us all. I mean, if you could beat your brothers, you were the best in the world, right? Well, not exactly, but you couldn't have told us that.

David was the oldest and by far the meanest. I can remember yard football games where he would purposely wait until Phillip, the youngest, or I ran the ball near the street so that he could tackle us onto the pavement instead of the grass. His game plan was simple: *Pound* them into submission! And for years he did just that. He never gave us an inch, and he forced us to be tougher than we thought we were capable of being.

Pain was never an issue for him. I can vividly remember a time when both of us screwed up and Dad was forced to spank us. Dad walked in the room with a two by four that at that moment looked like the largest piece of lumber these eyes had ever seen. David was first as he leaned over onto the bed like the professional that he was when it came to receiving punishment. Dad began to pound him so hard that I turned my head and began to cry for him. But after a couple of blows, I looked up at David and his face was fixed with a wry grin. He said to me, "What are you crying for?" in a voice that said this is no big deal at all. Dad saw that no pain was being inflicted on David, and so he didn't even bother to spank me, thank God. I knew from that point on that David was physically the toughest, meanest

My family has been there for me on and off the field. (Back row) My parents, Mike and Darlene. (Front row) David, me, and Phillip. *Courtesy of the author.*

person I had ever seen, and it was that toughness that he used against us that taught me the first lesson of being an athlete: every great athlete *must* have a mean streak.

Well, if you knew me, you would probably bet the house that a mean streak is nonexistent in these bones of mine. I've been described as shy, passive, quiet, and laid back by those who know me best. But any former teammate of mine can attest to my mean streak on the playing field. I think many of them were surprised and taken aback by my aggressiveness and flat-out meanness on the gridiron. And if you think I am bad, you should see Phillip. David was ten times tougher on Phillip than he was on me, and that's extremely evident in Phillip's hard-hitting style of play. He's the only person I know who can last two seasons at an SEC institution playing middle linebacker at only 200 pounds.

Obviously, growing up in our house was tough. Not through any fault of my parents, but rather from the competitive spirit that the three of us had. The competitiveness spilled over into all aspects of our daily lives. We fought over everything, as I'm sure happens in every household with three boys. We competed for superiority at video games, for who got to change the channels on the TV, and for who got to sit in the front seat of the car on the way to school. Everything we did was a challenge for supremacy. So when the time came for me to take my abilities and use them against others my age, there was no one close to my level.

Organized football began for me at the young age of five. Although I wanted to play when I was four, league rules would not allow me to start until I turned five years old. So as soon as they could, Mom and Dad took me up to Center Point Ball Park to register me for the upcoming season. The Alabama Youth Football League (AYFL) was set up by age and weight classes. Boys ages five through seven played together at a 70-pound weight limit. You played an eight-game regular season against other parks in the Birmingham area. Then there was a three-round playoff bracket culminating in a championship game played at a local high school. Each park had a total of six teams ranging from the 70-pound squad up to the 120-pound squad. Our park was a dominant force in the league. Numerous well known athletes came through Center Point Ball Park, such as Phillip Doyle, Craig Bryant, and Jay Barker, to name a few. Well, now it was my turn to lace up the cleats and shoulder pads to see if football was for me.

As a five-year-old playing on a team loaded with seven-year-olds, our coaches didn't give me much of a look. Although I was faster than everyone else on the Center Point Stallions, I became the center and defensive end, of all positions! Most of us had to play both ways because there were only 15 of us. We were known as the "Mean Fifteen." My neighbor and good friend Greg Miller was the quarterback, and we used to practice snaps in his front yard to make sure the center-quarterback exchange was perfected. I have no idea what our record ended up being that season, but I knew one thing: I loved to play this game.

It wasn't until my second season of football that I really began to understand how to play this game as it was supposed to be played. That season, the majority of my teammates and the team name moved into the next age and weight level, but because I was only six years old, I had to remain with the 70-pound squad under their new name, the Center Point Roughriders. I was now a year older, and we had a new coaching staff. The offensive coordinator was a gruff-sounding man named Tim Cole. I became the quarterback for the Roughriders, and with the one exception of Coach Bill Oliver, Tim Cole taught me more about football than any coach that I've ever been associated with, and I've been associated with some darn good ones.

That season was extremely memorable for me, but the fact that it was the first time that I was called a *champion* topped it off. We won the AYFL title by beating Huffman, our biggest rival, in overtime. For a young kid, just beginning to play the game, the success of winning a title gave me immense confidence and motivated me to be the best at the sport, year in and year out.

After that season, the Roughriders moved to the 80-pound level, and I was once again limited to the 70-pound level because of my age. But the majority of our coaches, including Coach Tim, stayed with my age group.

Coach Tim. I could write an entire book filled with Tim Cole stories. At the time, he worked for a cable company in Birmingham, and because of his job, he would always drive his large white cable truck to practice. I can vividly remember pulling into the ballpark, seeing that white truck, and thinking to myself, "Damn! Why couldn't someone's cable box have blown up today?" I knew that practice was going to be difficult, because he always made it especially difficult for me. He demanded from his six-year-old quarterback nothing less than perfection in games and even more so in practice. Did you catch that last line? Six years old! One, two, three, four, five, *six*! Perfection! I couldn't even pronounce perfection! But nonetheless, it was demanded of me on a daily basis, and I'm thankful for that. If Coach Tim had not come into my life, I would have been half the athlete that I am today. He came along at the perfect time in a young athlete's life and taught me how to push myself to achieve greatness.

Coach Tim was a huge Alabama fan, so much so that he would tell me constantly how great it would be to run onto the field wearing that "crimson helmet." He would later become Alabama's best recruiter. At home, Mom and Dad were big-time 'Bama fans, so I was surrounded with crimson and white stuff. In the second grade, I received a letter from Alabama coach Bill Curry. It congratulated my team on a tremendous championship season, as well as my individual success that season (2,572 yards and 64 touchdowns in 18 games). He also stated how much he appreciated my hard work in the classroom and how much he looked forward to me becoming a future Crimson Tider.

So naturally, I became a diehard Alabama fan through thick and thin. Iron Bowls meant the world to me. When Bo went over the top, I remember Dad throwing a stuffed football at the television and feeling sick for "my team." When Van Tiffin kicked the game-winning 52-yard field goal, I remember my entire family jumping for joy in the living room, probably one jump away from falling through our floor. I can say without caution that Alabama football had swept over me and was a driving force behind everything I did in my life, from age six on. I had developed an intense hatred of Auburn (or "Aubrin" as we used to pronounce it), but hey, I was from Birmingham. Isn't everyone in Birmingham an Alabama fan? Just joking.

Now seven years old, this would be my last year at the 70-pound level, and from here on out, I would move up through the league with my new team, the Center Point Gators. To make a long Little League career short, I played five more seasons with the Gators. We won the AYFL title every year. As a matter of fact, we lost only two games in five seasons. Our record was 70-something and two. And one of those losses was extremely controversial. We were beyond the description of dominant; we were a youth-league dynasty, the toast of the park, if you will, that still is talked about to this day. Needless to say, we had some major talent on our ball club. If we could have all stayed together throughout high school, there's not a doubt in my mind that we would have won the state championship. The lessons we learned from being Center Point Gators and from coaches like Tim Cole were immeasurable. They taught us the values of teamwork, discipline, character, and how to handle success. And because we were so successful, the area junior high coaches were grinning from ear to ear, just waiting to get their hands on us.

I actually began playing junior high football a year earlier than most of the kids my age. Instead of finishing my career at Center Point by playing with the 120-pound Gator team, I chose to play for my junior high team, the Erwin Eagles. I participated in Erwin's spring training while at Center Point

Elementary, so without question, it was pretty doggone tough. Because of time constraints, I had to take my football pants to school and change into them in the school bathroom every day at about 2:15 p.m. Mom would then check me out of school for the last half-hour and quickly drive me over to the junior high for practice. I was the only sixth grader from my elementary school who was crazy enough to do this, and I was one of only two sixth-graders who went through spring training that year. The other foolish sixth-grader was a guy named Jay Sanders, who became my best friend.

Junior high football obviously was very different from the park ball that I had played my entire life. For starters, age was a factor. I was playing with guys in the eighth and ninth grades, and not many seventh graders decided to play the first season of junior high ball. Also, I was introduced quite harshly to the weight room. I hadn't picked up weights in my entire life. But from looking around the locker room, it was evident I had to get stronger, even though physically I was already as tall or taller than most guys on the squad because I hit a growth spurt in sixth grade. Seven inches in three months! And lastly, there was an enormous change in the speed of the game. With all of these changes, I wondered, "Am I in over my head?"

Well, not exactly. I ended up starting on both sides of the ball, playing fullback on offense and cornerback on defense. But a seventh-grade starter was just too much for one parent in particular to take. The parent of my backup at cornerback (a ninth-grader) wrote a letter to the coaching staff saying how embarrassing and completely ludicrous it was to have a seventh-grader get so much playing time. I didn't know about the letter until my senior year in high school when some of my coaches jokingly shared this information with me.

TV TIMEOUT—Parents, let your kids' coaches *coach*. They *probably* know what they're doing! There's nothing more annoying than a parent who's always coaching from the stands. Teach your kids some discipline and maturity by holding your tongue at their sporting events. If you're always "fixing" the situation for your children, they'll never learn the lessons that sports can teach them.

I don't mean to tell you how to raise your children. It's just I've seen a lot of kids hate and even quit athletics simply because their parents were overbearing. Take that for what it's worth.

The next season I played quarterback and safety for the junior high team. Physically, I had gotten much stronger and was already looking forward to my ninth-grade year when finally I would be one of the oldest guys on the team.

Well, things didn't exactly happen as I had planned. Instead of being the oldest on the junior high team, I became the youngest player on the high school team. I was pulled up as a ninth grader to initially be the backup quarterback to the senior starter. Instead, I became a two-way starter at safety and tailback as a freshman.

My high school head coach was an inspiring leader named Hal Riddle. If his name sounds familiar, it is because he guided the Clay-Chalkville Cougars to the Class 6A state title in 1999 and currently is the head football coach for the Hewitt-Trussville Huskies. Coach Riddle is the greatest Christian man whom I have ever known. To have him as a head coach in high school was a tremendous privilege for us simply because of the type of man he was. In the four years I played for the man, he

Coach Hal Riddle, my high school football coach, became a role model for me while I played for him. What he taught me I took with me to college. *Courtesy of the author.*

never said a curse word. Never! And we all know how difficult teenagers can be. Aside from football—I believe he is an offensive genius—the man taught us about the facts of life. He taught us to be responsible, punctual, thoughtful, and honest and to be men of integrity. He was and is today a tremendous role model for me. So I say to Coach Riddle, "Thank you!"

The great coaching and character didn't by any means stop with the head man. It filtered down from Coach Riddle to his assistant coaches. Each coach at Erwin High School had a positive effect on my life, whether it was athletically, spiritually, or mentally through encouragement. My position coach in football, as well as my head basketball coach, Dale Patrick, is an incredible Christian, who still keeps in contact with my family and me to this day. My defensive coordinator and the head baseball coach, Johnny Metcalf, was the fiery one of the bunch; as one Plainsman to another, he still sends me e-mail messages. The coach who was the happiest following my eventual commitment to Auburn was Chris Moss. Coach Moss was my offensive position coach for my sophomore through senior years following my position change from tailback to wingback. He calls periodically to make sure all is well with Dana and me. The comedian of the group, Coach Jeff Estes, could always make me laugh no matter what. That may have been the most important quality of them all. They were a remarkable group of coaches, but more importantly, they were all fine Christian men, and I'm proud to call them my friends.

The memories and friendships made in high school are unforgettable and irreplaceable. From the ninth grade through my senior year, each team holds a special place in my heart, and friendships were made that will last a lifetime. Friends such as Jay Sanders, Jeff Hickman, and Christopher Martin made high school special and memorable for me, and I thought about them every time I suited up as an Auburn Tiger.

You know, after four years of college football, I've played in some big games as an Auburn Tiger, but every time a group of players gets together and starts talking football, it's the high school games that we always bring up. After all this time, I've figured out why that is. It's because high school football is football in its purest form. Football in high school is just a game and nothing more, and once you go through the political world of college football, the past becomes incredibly attractive.

My high school football career was a tremendous success thanks to many elements that came together for me. For starters, the good Lord blessed me with athletic talent, and I was always sure to give credit where credit was due. I had excellent coaches who were fine Christian men, who respected us enough

Brian Tribble, the "Voice of the Erwin Eagles" and a close friend of my family, and Dana share a moment at Homecoming my junior year. *Courtesy of the author.*

to teach us how to be not only great players, but also extraordinary men. I had tremendously talented teammates, who either threw a devastating block, zipped in a pass, or pressured a quarterback, which made me look better than I really was. Finally, I had my parents and a girlfriend constantly praying for me.

> ***TV TIMEOUT***—For everyone who has told me that my high school sweetheart would be just a passing relationship, I say to you thanks for the laughs and the motivation. You have helped me become a better husband to her!

What did all this mean for me, the high school football player? It meant being named to the Super All-State Team two consecutive years. It meant, on offense, 40 career touchdowns, and on defense 18 career interceptions. (I know what you're saying. "He could catch in high school! What happened?" Any former teammate of mine at Auburn can attest to my propensity to drop the easiest of interceptions.) It also meant All-American status and major college recognition.

The recruiting process is a funny thing. You hear so many different things from different people about what being recruited to play major college football is all about. To me, you make it as easy and fun or as difficult and miserable as you want—and for me it was extremely fun.

As I've already told you, I grew up a passionate Alabama fan. But something happened to me that really opened my eyes to that university on the eastern side of the state.

> **TV TIMEOUT**—This is a warning to Alabama fans who have never visited Auburn: All it took was one visit for me, and that was it. I fell in love!

I came to the Terry Bowden football camp the summer before my junior year of high school, and it was one of the wisest choices of my young life. It was the first time that I had been to Auburn and the first time that I had anything on my body that read AUBURN. However, there was an amazingly alluring, engaging feeling I got about the place that let me know that I had found home.

As a lifelong Alabama fan, I must admit that prior to my initial trip to Auburn the idea of wearing orange and blue did seem a bit whimsical to me. My parents didn't attend Alabama or Auburn, yet Alabama was always the household school of choice. Dad would tell me stories of guys like Darwin Holt, a defender whom, on occasion, Alabama coaches would not even allow to practice because he hit so hard and hurt too many people. We would visit the Bryant Museum and see all of the legendary figures who wore crimson and white. My Little League football coaches would even punish us if we dare wore orange and blue to practice with extra running after practice, even if the orange and blue had nothing to do with Auburn. Auburn was never given a fair chance to steal my heart as I had never even visited the campus, even though my grandparents live just 20 minutes from campus in Dadeville, Alabama.

But a crimson-slanted upbringing couldn't halt an Auburn invasion of my heart the first time I laid eyes on the place. To me, the rivalry between the two schools may have been fierce, but the campuses were incomparable, with Auburn the winner by a landslide. I know I had to have been blushing my entire trip at that football camp because for my entire life I had hated and judged something I never even knew, and that was somewhat embarrassing. I had fallen for Auburn, and there was no turning back.

I kept my feelings for Auburn to myself, because my family and the majority of my friends and coaches were Alabama fans. So throughout the entire recruiting process, most people thought that I was for sure an Alabama lean. Maybe on the outside, but never in the heart.

I received my first letters of interest from Florida State University and Notre Dame on the same day in 10th grade. I can remember Coach Riddle placing the letters in my hand. I began to swell up with pride as I looked down at that shiny, gold helmet on the envelope from the Fighting Irish. I can also remember how quickly Coach Riddle brought me back down to reality by telling me that I probably just made some mailing list and would more than likely be receiving more mail. *Instantaneous deflation!* Thanks, Coach, I appreciate the vote of confidence.

Well, he was right about one thing: I did receive some more mail. Over the next three years, I bet I got a few thousand letters from colleges all over the United States. I saved every letter, and they sit today in the basement of my parents' home in Chelsea, Alabama.

Once coaches could begin to contact me by phone, things began to really get interesting and very funny. For the life of me I cannot remember the coach's name, but a coach from Stanford University was really after me early. He gave me the spiel about the prestige of Stanford and how they were forced to recruit guys like me from coast to coast because of the academic standards of the Cardinal. He then proceeded to tell me that in order to get into Stanford, I was going to have to do better on my ACT. Now, I'm not the smartest guy in the world, but I did manage to graduate from high school with a 4.3 GPA. My ACT score was a mediocre 25, but that was far higher than what every other school in the nation demanded. I told the man "sorry" and that I was through with the ACT. And that was the last time I heard from Stanford. With academic standards so stringent, how do they stay competitive?

It was becoming quite clear just where my future lay for two reasons: the allure of Auburn and Alabama's lack of interest. Going into the whole mess, I had a game plan. First, I wanted to play in the Southeastern Conference, the toughest football conference in all the land. Next, I wanted to stay in the state of Alabama for obvious reasons (close to home, great traditions, etc.). So in other words, I had it narrowed down to two before the recruiting process ever even began. With Auburn's growing interest and Alabama's lack thereof, choosing a college was probably the easiest decision that I've made in my life.

Rodney Allison, Auburn's intense offensive coordinator and running backs coach, recruited me for Auburn, and he did an excellent job. He called once or twice a week and just talked to me about whatever was on his mind. It really came natural to him, and he made me feel quite comfortable. He was a major factor in my decision to come to the Plains, and I miss him a lot.

But better than Coach Allison's phone calls was the time Coach Bowden came to my church, Centercrest Baptist, to preach, perfectly timing the trip smack-dab in the middle of recruiting season. I knew then that these guys must really want me for Coach Bowden to give a sermon on my behalf. I say on my behalf, but Jason Standridge, the state's top-rated quarterback, was also there. We committed to Auburn together, so Coach Bowden killed two birds with one stone.

TV TIMEOUT—You think I'm joking, but if some college coaches read this last paragraph, they'll be the guest speakers in churches all across America. They'll do whatever it takes! Watch your local church marquees.

There is no way I could end this discussion on recruiting without two incredible stories. Many people are under the impression that most recruits get cars, clothes, money, and other merchandise in order to commit to a particular school. Well, from what I saw throughout the recruiting process, this happens very seldom and never happened to me. But two interesting things did happen to yours truly.

The first was a coach who called me every single day. About the only thing this man did not promise me was a position on the staff. One day he'd say, "You'll be a freshman starter, guaranteed." The next day, "Oh, your girlfriend's a cheerleader? She'd make a fabulous cheerleader at our school." Ring... Ring... "Hello." "Rob, you want to be a physical therapist? No problem, we'll get you in PT school for sure." The promises became so ridiculous that he eliminated his school as a choice for me. But, hey, Coach, I could use a job now; are you still cutting deals?

The second story is even more comical than the first. A health teacher at my school got a phone call one evening from a prominent alumnus from his alma mater. Their topic of conversation was about my interest in their school, and he asked what it would take to get me to commit to his school. Well, because I kept this particular teacher in the know about who was contacting me, he knew that this particular school had not even sent a letter and signing day was just around the corner. So jokingly, my teacher told him that it was going to take a brand-new red Dodge Ram. Then he continued, "I take that back. It's going to take two brand-new red Dodge Rams, because I want one, too." He remained quiet to see how this man responded to his wisecrack. Then, after about a 10-second pause, the alumnus said, "Well, let me see what I can do." What? My teacher couldn't believe it. For one, it was his alma mater that we're talking about here, and he also wanted no part of a foul deal. Finally, he respected my family and me enough to know not to make deals on my behalf. He let the poor man have it. So basically, this school never sent me a letter, *but* a red Dodge Ram was a definite possibility. Shoot, they probably couldn't afford expensive paper and envelopes after loaning out cars!

With my parents by my side, I sign my national letter of intent
to play for Auburn and begin my journey into the world of college football. *Courtesy of the author.*

But other than that, the recruiting process was straightfor-
ward and interesting. Most schools were very professional about
the entire procedure, and the different institutions had plenty to
offer. But as I said before, I had it narrowed down to two institutions from the very beginning, and lucky for me, I chose the
Tigers.

TV TIMEOUT—On October 25, 1996, the Erwin
Eagles traveled to Morris, Alabama, to take on the
undefeated, fifth-ranked team in Class 5A, the
Mortimer Jordan Blue Devils. En route to a 21-7 victory over our newest area rival, I managed to score
touchdowns by receiving, rushing, and returning an

interception, and I also recovered a fumble caused by my brother, Phillip. I enjoyed one of my best performances before the watchful eyes of Curly Hallman, the University of Alabama defensive back coach. Obviously, Coach Hallman left Morris, Alabama, dreadfully unimpressed, because I never heard from him again, confirming my instinct that Auburn was the place for me.

CHAPTER 2

New Beginnings

Rob Pate was an outstanding high school athlete. He excelled in football, basketball, and baseball. He was an All-State athlete in football and baseball, he was the Class 5A Bryant Jordan Scholar Athlete in 1997, and he earned a football scholarship to Auburn University. Those are pretty impressive credentials, but they pale in comparison to the kind of young man Rob is.

Rob was a leader. He led by example. He led in the weight room, in the classroom, in the locker room, and on the field. He pushed himself. He was always first in every conditioning drill. Not only did he get better, but he also made his teammates better. Nobody ever had to tell him twice to do anything. He listened! During the four years I coached him, I cannot remember a time when I was addressing our team that he did not have his eyes right on me. He was disciplined. He did things the way he was told to do them, every time. He studied regularly on the bus, in the gym, in the locker room, and at home. He used his time wisely. He was very respectful to teachers, coaches, opponents, and teammates. He was also very humble. He always credited his teammates, his coaches, and most importantly his God for helping him accomplish so much. Rob is a classy young man with a lot of character.

Hal Riddle
Head Coach
Erwin High School
1993-1998

My roommate Whit Smith (No. 42) and I stand inside Room 124 in Sewell Hall before our first Auburn Fan Day. *Courtesy of the author.*

The summer before I had to leave for school utterly flew by. I had a job working for the Pepsi Company, which was an extremely arduous task. I would get there at 6:00 a.m. and work until about 3:00 p.m. I would then leave and drive straight to Wallace's Super Gym in Center Point to work out. From there, I would drive over to the high school to run sprints at the track. It would be dark before I finally got home, but in my eyes, it all had to be done. The hard work paid off enormously for me; I got much stronger and was in superb condition. I was ready to leave for the Plains. Or so I thought!

By far, the most difficult thing was having to leave home. I remember the day just like it was yesterday. All of the sudden, all of the hype was over, and I was *actually* leaving for Auburn.

What were my thoughts? Well, really I just wanted to help out the team in any way I could. Perhaps I would be a special teams player and hopefully be a solid backup. There was no way of knowing. What I did know was the "experts" didn't think that I would amount to that much. I was overshadowed by the likes of Demontray Carter, Herman Banks, Meiko Collier, and Asa Francis, and not much was expected from me when I stepped onto the field for the first time.

TV TIMEOUT—What is it exactly that makes football "experts" so much more knowledgeable about the sport than you and me? Well, let me tell you, *not a thing*. If my career had turned out as they brilliantly prophesized, I *might* have played my senior season. Of the four teammates in the previous paragraph who were far sexier recruits than I was, none lasted more than two seasons at Auburn.

The opportunity to play for Coach Bill Oliver was the highlight of my career at Auburn. I was well aware of Coach Oliver's success at Alabama, and to have a defensive legend as my position coach and defensive coordinator was the final factor that convinced me to go to Auburn. In my mind and many others, no one worked harder or knew more about how to play great defense than Coach Oliver. He was the best teacher of the game for whom I ever played. I learned more about football in the two years I played for Coach Oliver than I ever imagined possible.

His defensive schemes were incredibly difficult to learn and required numerous days of study, especially for the safeties. It was up to us in the "back end," as he used to say, to make sure that we were always in the correct defense. Because so much was required of the safeties physically and mentally in Coach Oliver's 3-4 defensive scheme, it was, in my opinion, the toughest of all positions to play. Even so, I, especially as a true freshman, prospered uncommonly throughout the summer.

I came to practice every day eager to learn and was literally in awe of Coach Oliver. I listened to every word he uttered and tried desperately to keep up in the meetings and film sessions. Football, as I had known it, had been transformed into something that seemed to be larger than life. Playbooks, as thick as world almanacs and more bewildering than the Book of Revelation, became the norm. Meetings starting at 5:15 a.m. were absolutely brutal. The most minuscule details never went unnoticed. I had never seen anything like it before.

I knew from the outset that in order to get a chance to play, I had to learn the defense quickly. Coach Oliver didn't make this an easy task either, because he was making me learn both the free and strong safety positions at the same time. Those two positions were, by far, the most difficult and involved positions

Coach Bill Oliver taught me more about football than I thought was possible. He is a remarkable man and coach. *Courtesy of Auburn University.*

on the field. Learning just one of the positions was mentally exhausting in and of itself. It took many players four years, their entire college careers, to learn their responsibilities at the safety spot. But here he had me doing double duty, learning two times what was expected of all others on our squad. And guess what happened? I learned the defense twice as fast because of this. You may ask, "Well, why was he so tough on you?" Coach Oliver knew what he was doing with me the entire time. He was grooming me to run his defense for the next four seasons.

Being able to swing from free safety to strong safety allowed me to see what was taking place on both sides of the defense. I saw how each safety fit into the defense, and things began making sense. And because I could play both safety positions, I doubled my value as a backup.

The other guys in the defensive backfield could tell that I was making enormous strides for being a true freshman. In particular, the two starting safeties, Martavius Houston, or "Dooney" as we called him, and Brad Ware surprisingly took me under their wings. I thought for sure that they would not appreciate the fact that I was picking up on things at such a fast pace and was a potential threat to their established starting roles. But, no, it was amazingly quite the contrary. They told me in private what I was doing wrong and how I needed to fix it. They made it possible for me to ask them questions and not worry about a verbal lashing for not remembering something from a meeting. But most importantly, they accepted me as one of their teammates, as an equal. They didn't see race or personal differences as a reason to not embrace the new kid on the block. I learned a lot from them in those first few weeks, and they became great friends in the short time we played together. They easily could have made things difficult for me every day, but instead they welcomed my presence and athleticism, making the transition for me all the more comfortable and fulfilling.

Away from the football field and the athletic complex, I was learning how to live without my fiancée. *Fiancée?* Yes! I had asked Dana to marry me the last weekend of high school in front of my entire church congregation.

> *TV TIMEOUT*—The response from several of my new teammates upon telling them how I had asked Dana to marry me—"*Man*, that took *steel* balls!" Yeah, fellas, it did! But it turned out to be perfect, and we've got it all on video.

Although Dana would be coming to school in the fall (end of September), things were definitely tough on the two of us because we were apart.

Dana and I met in the eighth grade on Homecoming night. We were with other dates but happened to be together in a group of eight that shared a stretch limousine. She immediately caught my eye, and I managed to snare hers as well. By the next Thursday, we were the talk of the junior high as the new couple of the week. And now, boy, how those weeks have piled up.

So as you can probably tell, Dana and I spent an awful lot of time together, and not being there for one another was something that was grinding for us both.

My new home was room 124 in Sewell Hall. Sewell Hall is the athletic dorm where all freshman scholarship players must live in their first year on campus. All that this room consisted of was oversized bunk beds, a set of shelves, two desks, a shower, and a toilet. All of this was crammed into a room that two football players were supposed to live in. I was supposed to room with Jason Standridge, a friend from my Center Point football days and the state's top quarterback prospect. Jason also was one of the best high school pitchers in the United States and was drafted as the last pick of the first round by the Tampa Bay Devil Rays in 1997. He decided baseball was the best route for him. Great for Jason, but not so great for Rob. I had lost my roommate before I ever stepped foot on campus.

Lucky for me though, I did have a roommate when I showed up that day. Whit Smith, aka "Fat Head," was my new acquaintance, and I couldn't have had a better person to share a box with! He was a PK, preacher's kid, and it took virtually every verse of scripture and each memorized sermon he could muster up to get us through those first months. You got to know someone really well, sometimes a bit too well, when you shared such close quarters. He would have to put up with me talking to Dana incessantly, and I would have to tolerate his country-boy accent and late-night appetite. But we had a ton of good times in that room playing PlayStation, prank-calling people, making hilarious answering machine messages, and, of course, talking football. We developed a friendship that will last to death, and room 124 Sewell Hall will never be the same.

Back on the practice field, Coach Oliver was telling me that I was doing things he had never seen a freshman do. The pre-season scrimmages went well for me, and it was evident I was making progress. He would even go as far as telling some of the upperclassmen that they could learn from watching me! That was an awkward position to be in. I had been practicing now for about three weeks, and he was telling guys who had been there for years to do things like I did them. As two-a-days ended, I was on a couple of special teams and was starting on the nickel packages.

The end of two-a-days also brought one of the football team's favorite Auburn traditions, *rookie night*. Rookie night is when the entire team—players, coaches, managers, and trainers—meets in the team meeting room, and the newcomers entertain the upperclassmen with skits. It's a fun time because it signals the end of two-a-day practices, and the skits are amazingly hilarious. Now, there were a couple of rules you must follow in rookie night: 1) Groups could be no larger than five; 2) if you were funny, you got to stay in the room and watch the rest of the skits; 3) if you were not funny, well, you got *barraged* with the tape balls that every person in the room had and you must leave the room and remain outside until rookie night was over.

I came up with a ridiculous idea for a skit. I thought it would be funny if I rapped "Rice, Rice, Baby!" a takeoff of Vanilla Ice's "Ice, Ice, Baby!" I recruited three other guys, Demontray Carter, Tavarreus Pounds, and Roderick Chambers, to dance behind me as I rapped. It sounded like a great plan. I knew they would love it, and we would get to watch everyone else make fools of themselves.

Well, things didn't go as planned to say the least. I got the first line of the song out of my mouth before Dameyune Craig stood up and started to boo. I thought my life was over. Every player in the auditorium began firing tape bombs in our direction at the speed of light. As we hightailed it toward the door, tape pounded me in the back of the head. When we finally managed to open the large double doors, the amount of tape that came flying out of the auditorium would have given any trainer within eyeshot a heart attack.

TV TIMEOUT—You may be wondering, "Why would the trainers care if tape was being wasted in mass quantities?" Well, because apparently during my time at Auburn, tape was worth more than gold. We were told that we couldn't spat our cleats before games because Auburn couldn't *afford* the tape! That's right, tape was just too expensive a commodity in Auburn's *multimillion-dollar* budget. No money for tape. Give me a break.

Something else that markedly annoyed me was the repulsive apparel we received from Frank Cox, Auburn's perennial equipment manager. Getting a new pair of gloves or some new pants for practice from Frank was the equivalent of getting a meaningful tax cut from a modern-day Democrat—it wasn't going to happen. I never knew who to be angry at—Frank for not giving us the things we needed to be comfortable on the playing field or Auburn for, I'm sure, giving him a ludicrously limited budget to work with. Nonetheless, we were forced to go without at an institution where that should never happen.

We went to class every day and saw the *ladies' tennis team* or *women's basketball team* wearing brand-name apparel while we were issued items that I wouldn't even wear in the confines of my house, let alone out in public. Never once were we given a name-brand item like our counterparts in other sports. Yet, I would bet the income from football pays for what they sport every day in class. Is that fair?

To say the least, we were terrible, but I'm sure we presented a challenging target for tape-bomb practice. It was most definitely a humbling experience for me. But after all of the skits were presented and all of the laughs were over, all newcomers were humbled one last time. The seniors made the entire freshman class come to the front of the auditorium to sing the fight song. Of course, in the midst of all of the older guys as well as all of the coaches, no one wanted to start the fight song and only a handful of guys even knew it. After we finished our miserable rendition of the song, they all booed and then stood on their feet. Dameyune counted aloud, "ONE, TWO! ONE, TWO, THREE, FOUR!" Then, the entire team ecstatically sang the fight song with such pride and conviction that we all stood there in shock. I had goose bumps covering my entire body. From that moment on, I realized that Auburn football was much bigger than any one person or any one game. It was an everlasting spirit, a respect for those who had come before us, and a love of the school. I saw all of this in their faces and heard it in their demonstrative voices. These guys loved Auburn and were proud of its tradition. I embraced it that night and will carry it with me forever.

The time had come to begin my career at Auburn. We were to kick off the season on ESPN against the Virginia Cavaliers on the road in Charlottesville, Virginia. I was ready for the game. But I wasn't as prepared for the trip!

TV TIMEOUT—My parents drove to every game I ever played as an Auburn Tiger. Whether it was right down the road in Birmingham's Legion Field or all the way to Fayetteville, Arkansas, they made the trek on our nation's interstates to see me play. One of their longest hauls was to watch my first game ever, in Charlottesville, Virginia, a 12-hour journey from Birmingham to the historic homeland of Thomas

Jefferson. As my mom and dad strolled the campus of the University of Virginia prior to Tiger Walk and the beginning of my collegiate career, I can imagine an extensive realm of emotions flooded their minds that afternoon—excitement, anxiety, wonder, confusion?

Yes, confusion. Walking to the stadium, adorned in orange and blue for the first time in their lives, complete with an enormous "My son is #31" pin, a fellow Auburn tailgater passing in the opposite direction passionately acknowledged my parents with "War Eagle!" Expecting a proud, energized "War Eagle" response from my parents, the Auburn man was I'm sure thrown for one of the biggest loops of his life. In what can only be characterized properly as an enormous brain cramp on the part of my mother, her response to "War Eagle" was what it had been her entire life—"Roll Tide!"

Mom took a few steps before she even realized what she had just said, it was just old hat to her. It was like riding a bike, once you learn you never forget. Embarrassed by what she said, she didn't even turn around to correct herself.

I'm certain there's an Auburn man walking around somewhere confident that Rob Pate's mom was one of two things—a drunk or an Alabama fan. The first I assure you has never been the case. The second—well, it would take a game or two to perfect the Auburn salutation procedure. I'll just attribute the slip of tongue to that long trip.

Sitting in that small, cramped seat and trembling from my unruly nerves, I prayed that the Lord would see me through this. For the first time in my life, I sat helplessly in a plane on the runway pondering what was about to take place. I just knew that something horrible was going to happen. Would anyone even remember me if we crashed? What if I got sick in front of my teammates? They'd never let it die down. Some of the older guys on the team made sure they sat around me so that they could be amused by my fear. It wasn't that I was panicking, yelling, or anything of the sort, but what I did was I entered my shell. You know, *your* own world, in which all distractions are blocked out of your mind. Once the plane was in the air, I was fine—except for Cole Cubelic yelling, "We're gonna die!" when we hit the first small air pocket. But eventually, the plane landed, and a championship season was about to begin.

TV TIMEOUT—In my four years of college football, I became accustomed to and even enjoyed flying. But did you know that on November 14, 1970, a plane carrying the Marshall Thundering Herd football team crashed, killing the entire squad. How awful that must have been for the family and friends of all who perished in that dreadful accident.

Before I knew it, I was standing in the tunnel, staring up into the crowd in absolute amazement. Our white jerseys and white pants were shining brightly because the sun had fallen and the bright lights of prime-time college football glared. I had just been through my first Tiger Walk, my first pregame warmup, and my first pregame prayer with the defensive backs. The time had come. I was standing next to Dooney in the tunnel when he began to shout, "F--- the ACC, we're the SEC! Let's show 'em how we play ball down South!"

Then, I remember the calming spirit of the Lord came over me in a way that had never happened in all my years of football. He reassured me that all of the hard work was about to pay off, and instantly, all butterflies were gone.

On our first offensive drive, the offense went backward instead of forward, and our punter was forced to punt the ball from our own two-yard line. The punt was blocked in the end zone, and Jaret Holmes managed to fall on the ball, resulting in a safety for the Cavaliers. On the ensuing possession, the Cavs took the ball inside our five-yard line, looking to jump out to a quick 9-0 lead and dampen our initial intensity. On third down from our two-yard line, I was given the call to enter the ballgame. I was excited yet nervous because I realized the importance of the play; I sprinted onto the field just as Virginia was breaking their huddle. I, a wide-eyed 18-year-old true freshman, took my place on the edge of the line of scrimmage. Suddenly, the flow of the backfield was in my direction. Virginia was running the option right at me. Somehow, I managed to take on the block of their 260-pound fullback while maintaining leverage on the ball. As the quarterback, Aaron Brooks, pitched the ball to Thomas Jones, their talented tailback, I dove at the back, causing the pitch to end up on the ground. Brad Ware picked up the fumble and returned it up the near sideline to the 20-yard line. With our backs against the wall, we had held strong. It was my first play as an Auburn Tiger and one of the biggest of my career. Coach Oliver said after the game that he had never, in all his years of coaching, seen a true freshman make that kind of play.

TV TIMEOUT—When I first began in college football, I couldn't believe how ridiculously sensitive the policy makers had become in regard to penalizing celebration. I mean penalizing a man for making a circus catch and darting 80 yards for a touchdown because he salutes the student section or tosses the ball a bit too hard to the ground is absurd to me. And here's why.

Invision yourself in a foursome, laying two on a par four, just shy of the 18th green. You sink your chip shot from 30 yards out, and what do you do? Well, you meekly walk over to your golf cart, gently return the pitching wedge to your bag, and maybe even grin to the others in your group. *Yeah, right.* You howl, scream, and jump for joy. You probably even break into a little dance you've created only for shots like that. Now, if you do that on a golf course with only three pairs of eyes witnessing your marvelous feat, imagine what we feel like making a great play in front of 86,000 people.

There are those who celebrate only to bring attention to themselves and that should get a flag every time. But on most occasions, guys are just excited that their hard work has allowed them the opportunity to make a terrific play for their team. Don't penalize players for respectfully having fun! They've worked their tails off endlessly for those few moments of grandeur. Let them enjoy it!

We ended up beating Virginia that night, 28-19. I played about 30 snaps and graded out 100 percent. Because of the way

I played, along with problems at cornerback, I found myself starting the second week against Ole Miss in my first home game and conference contest.

I continued to play well, and we continued to win football games on the arm of Dameyune Craig. Before I knew it, we were 4-0 and about to travel to Columbia, South Carolina, to take on the South Carolina Gamecocks. Things couldn't have been better. I was the starting safety for the unbeaten Auburn Tigers. I was living the dream that seemed to be destined for me.

But then, something happened that made it all seem not as important and completely changed my life and the lives of hundreds forever. It was Thursday night, and Whit and I lay in our

My parents as Auburn fans after a game. *Courtesy of the author.*

dorm room laughing and joking with Jay Sanders, my best friend from high school. We stayed up late that rainy night talking about how far we had come in such a short period. Laughter filled the tiny room as Whit and I reenacted all of the comical stories from two-a-days and rookie night for Jay. It was really the first night that we had stayed up late and just talked about whatever was on our minds. This continued until a little before 1:00 a.m., when Jay left for his apartment.

We were in high spirits for several reasons that night. Practice was over for the week; we had only one more class to attend in the morning, and then I could concentrate on the trip to Columbia. I was looking forward to the game and the chance to run our record to 5-0. Whit was heading home to Cordele, Georgia, for the weekend. We were content and cheerful.

I'll never forget what happened next as long as I'm breathing. I felt a hand on my head as I lay in my bed on the top bunk. I heard someone sobbing loudly, and I thought it all to be a dream. Again, I felt the hand on my head and then my name was whispered in a rough, cracked voice, "Rob." I opened my eyes, only to make out a silhouette of someone standing there. I looked at my watch to see what time it was—4:00 a.m.

As I scrambled to find a light to see who was there and what he wanted, I recognized Jay's voice. When I turned on the light, I saw his face, which was full of pain and bright red from crying, and immediately I knew something terrible had happened. I began to tear up, knowing something horrific had taken place. I asked him, "What happened?" He said in weakened voice, "Man, Rob, it's awful! Brian was murdered! He was shot in the head at church!"

I asked him how he knew—he said word traveled from Birmingham, and he had received a call just a short time ago. Those were the only words spoken until sunrise, as we both sat in the room, me in the desk chair and Jay in the floor, crying our eyes out.

"So who was Brian?" you may be thinking. Brian Tribble was the heart and soul of my hometown of Center Point. He was the minister of music at my church, where he worked with my mother, who was the church secretary. Brian was also the public address announcer for all of my football games in high school, where he was known as "Voice of the Erwin Eagles." There is just no way I can describe to you what an amazing person Brian was because my words do him an utter injustice. He is the type of person who only comes along once in a lifetime. He could fill a room with laughter or sweep it to its feet with a voice straight from heaven. He loved me like a brother, and the feeling was mutual. He was such a special person in Dana's and my life that we had asked him that summer before we left for the Plains to marry us when the time came. He was so touched that we had asked him that he cried right in front of us.

Brian was also instrumental in my successful transition to Auburn. He had written me a letter a week and had filled them with much-needed humor, as well as inspirational messages. His letters had gotten me through some extremely difficult nights when practice had not gone that well and home seemed so far away. He had told me a million times how much he loved to watch me play. Brian had seen me play as an Auburn Tiger just one time, five days before his senseless murder, in a game against Central Florida, and wrote me about it.

October 2, 1997
From the incredibly fertile imagination of Brian Tribble,

I can't begin to tell you what a thrill it was for me to see you come off the field, go to the sidelines, and have somebody hand you

Brian Tribble was the minister of music at my church when he was murdered in 1997. Here he is with his two oldest daughters, Katelyn and McKinley. *Courtesy of the author.*

*the headset! But please Rob, dear God, tell Dana I would appreci-
ate it if she would not call you during the game. You've got enough
to think of with everything else...waitaminute, you're mom's telling
me it was Oliver talking to you...and you were getting chewed out.
Well then, never mind.*

*I really enjoyed myself Saturday, and it's so easy to see why peo-
ple fall in love with that place. From the Tiger Walk, to the game
itself, then you guys coming out and everybody and their brother
waiting on the players as they walk back to Sewell Hall, it was
great. And I really enjoyed finally meeting Whit and thank you
both for signing Jake Scott's ball, he's slept with it every night since
he got it. The funny thing is, I used to think that Charline
(Harbison) was the most rabid Auburn fan I had ever met. Well,
she ain't even close!*

*I've just been handed a copy of today's paper and there is a big
quote from you. "The scariest moment before last week was at LSU
and seeing the hole open up and Cecil Collins coming straight at
me. Then last week, here comes Daunte Culpepper running through
a hole by himself. Those are some big guys and they bring it with
them."*

*Bring what? IT? What is IT? Do I have to start writing your
quotes for you? "Yeah, he was big, but I whipped his a..." never
mind. Your mom just hit me in the back of the head.*

*Well, you guys smoke Carolina. I will be in Washington at the
Promise Keepers rally, but I'm taking a radio so I can find out how
you guys did. Tell Whit everybody says hi and we are all bringing
IT with us.*

The game was the last time I ever saw him.

I remember in the wee hours of that dreadful morning that
I had to see if the information that Jay had received was indeed
accurate. I tried to convince myself that maybe someone was

misinformed, maybe they had heard wrong, and perhaps Brian was still alive. Whit, who was awakened by our grieved outburst, suggested I call my parents, and so I dialed our phone number. (Because my house was maybe 300 yards from the church, my parents would know the truth.) When David answered the phone, I knew at that moment it was all true. At home, none of us had telephones in our rooms, so I discerned by his being out of bed at 6:00 a.m. that they already knew the gloomy news. With a trembling voice, all I could manage to say was, "David." He didn't have the strength to even respond; he just handed the phone to Mom. "Rob?" she said in a staggered tone that told me the worst was inevitable. All I could manage to ask my mother, who worked six days a week with Brian, her best friend, was, "Is it true?"

She confirmed that Brian was found dead in the back of the church offices a little after 3:00 a.m. that Friday morning. Brian had been at the church to help prepare breakfast for a men's group leaving for a Promise Keepers rally in Washington D.C. when he had startled a burglar robbing a Coke machine. He died doing God's work and never made it to D.C.

Now, I had to break the news to my fiancée. I called Dana in her dorm room at about 6:30 a.m. I told her to meet me outside in five minutes. "I've got some terrible news." She demanded to know right then, on the phone, what had taken place, but I insisted on telling her face to face. When Jay and I pulled up to Dana's dorm, she was already waiting for us in the parking lot. When we stepped out of the truck, she saw two distraught, confused teenagers, who had just lost a great friend, and now she was about to fall into the same miserable category. I put my arms around her to comfort her as much as possible before I had to tell her the most sickening news. With tears streaming down both of our faces, I whispered to her that Brian had been murdered. She almost passed out. She fell onto the grass in the courtyard of the Quad Dorms grieved with sadness. My heart broke for her.

October 3, 1997
Master P
Rob Shock

Bubba,

I was going to write you a letter anyway, but after this morning I was going to make sure I got this to you before you left. I'm not good sometimes at expressing, but I want you to know I'm mighty proud of you. You came in as just another freshman, and now you're starting for the Auburn Tigers. Through the practices, games, interviews, and stories written about you, you never change. You are one of only a few people who could handle these past two months as you have. Life has just hit you with circumstances you never could have imagined, but nothing you can't overcome. I know your thoughts will be back home this weekend. Remember Brian, and all the good times you shared. Remember the way he looked and spoke and how much he loved Rob Pate. I only knew Brian for a short time, but I was able to see what made him so special. I also believe that he'll be right with you tomorrow during the game. He loves you, and he loves to watch you play football. But not just play, but play with heart and compassion because that is how he lived, with heart and compassion. So do what Brian would want you to do. Go out and live life and play ball to the fullest. Brian will never miss a Rob Pate game, and Rob Pate will never forget Brian. Enjoy the game, and when you get back, I'll be here waiting to see ya and babble your head off. You WILL PLAY A GREAT GAME! I MEAN A GREAT GAME! I know it will be hard, but try to relax, and play your game tomorrow. You get your first of many interceptions. Good luck! W.I.N.

Love,
Whit (Smith)

With the death of Brian controlling my every thought, I boarded a Delta jet later that morning bound for Columbia and a clash with the Gamecocks. Here I was 18 years old, away from home for the first time in my life, and about to play an SEC football game the morning after a close family friend was taken from this earth. I was scatterbrained and brokenhearted as I lay in my hotel bed that night in South Carolina. Normally, I would be enjoying a movie with the team at a local movie theater, just like every other Friday night before our games, but tonight I just couldn't face my teammates and coaches.

I was pissed off that my loving, caring, kind God could take the life of a man who was a champion for His cause. Why didn't God shield Brian from harm's way? Where was his guardian angel? I was filled with questions, with pain, with anger, and with sorrow. I wept for his wife, Roxanne, and their four small children. I felt so helpless and far away.

October 2, 1997

Dear Rob,

Whit just called me and told me about the tragic death of your minister and friend. I'm so sorry, it's so senseless and we can't understand why this could happen to such a godly person. There's just a lot of sick and evil people in this world that don't care about anybody but themselves.

Rob, it's going to take some time, prayers, and God's grace to get you on the other side of this. You'll never forget or completely get over the loss of your friend, but God will provide you the strength to go on with your life. Now, you will look at life a lot different and see how precious every day is. God, and your friend, want you to go on. Now you can live your life for him too, through your Christian walk your friend can live on through you. His influence in your life will always be visible, his ministry doesn't stop—it gets to be revealed through you and the many other lives he touched.

I wish I could give you some answers to the "why" questions you'll have, but we cannot always know. We have to trust God in a time like this. His heart is broken too. He'll help you one day at a time to grow from this horrible tragedy. You'll know the power of His grace like never before and how we should make the most of every day for God's glory.

Please know that I am praying for you, Dana, your family, and your church family. I can only promise you one thing—God will be there for you in a marvelous way. He loves you very much and wants you to live for Him.

Always see your friend in heaven walking with the Lord Jesus Christ. And never forget, you'll be able to be reunited with him one day. If you can get a picture of him to have with you in the dorm room, let it remind you of his interest, love, and impact on your life—and let it remind you of the life you can live to carry on his ministry!

Let yourself grieve, it hurts. You have a great support group to help you as you will help them in the days ahead when they need you. Thanks for being a good friend to Whit, he recognizes that God brought ya'll together.

Looking forward to seeing you soon!

Peace and grace,
John (Whit's father)

Whit and me after a loss. On my left wristband are the initials
B.T., my tribute to my great friend. *Courtesy of the author.*

It was my parents' intention to not tell me about Brian until after the ballgame. Even with all of this taking place just one day before the game, my parents still made the trip to Columbia to watch me play. That tells you the character of my extraordinary parents. At Tiger Walk before the game, I could tell that they had been crying and their tears were contagious to me.

Before the game, I dedicated the rest of my athletic career to Brian and wrote his initials, B.T., on my wristbands. Those wristbands were a reminder to play the game like it's supposed to be played: with heart, with desire, and with passion. I did it to remember Brian and to remember how much he loved to watch me play. I did it so that in the fourth quarter of a brutal, hard-fought battle, I wouldn't forget my source of determination and inspiration. That gesture to his memory was short-lived. Later, I was told I could not wear them because there was a rule that prohibited players from writing anything on their wristbands—all players must be dressed exactly the same. How that simple action impaired the progression of a football game in any way is still an unsolved mystery to me. Nonetheless, at the season's end, I took my wristbands from that game against South Carolina and placed them at Brian's headstone. I believe he'll be wearing them when he greets me someday in heaven.

October 8, 1997

Rob,

I wanted to write you a few weeks ago to say thanks for spending time with Alec after the Ole Miss game, but with a new baby coming time was difficult to find. Now the words are difficult to find. We lost a tremendous friend, but we must go on with life. I know these days are very tough away from family, but stay focused on what God has given you. The past few days have made me feel as if I was walking around in the dark. I expect you feel much the same. Today I ran across a piece of God's Word that lifted my spirit a bit. Micah 7:8 'When I fall down as we are now the Lord will lift us up. Even in dark times God is with us and will light our paths.' At least that is my paraphrase of the verse. It is strange how much more we lean on God in these times. We should always depend on Him to light the darkness! My prayer is that in some way this letter will lift your spirit as writing it has lifted mine. When I stop and talk about all the great and fun things Brian did for others, you, and me, I know that he is now doing them in heaven. As part of his legacy I feel I need to become an encourager to others. He always encouraged me and we need, no must, carry on encouraging and praying for one another. Brian often told me how proud he was of you and how excited he was for you (even though you were playing at my school and not his). I hope you like the picture that I put in here. War Eagle!

In Christ,
Bartley (Brown)

Brian was special, and his ministry lives on through many today. I made a promise to myself to mention Brian's life whenever I speak at churches.

Our church bulletin put it best:

Brian Tribble was an angel without a halo, a minister without credentials, a worker with youth who never grew up, a music director that could not read music. But when he sang, heaven paused and there was the applause of men, and the rustle of angel wings.

He was a great father, super husband, hard worker, committed Christian.

Brian, we will miss you, but we'll never forget you, and never stop loving you. Thanks for the wonderful memories.

Yes Brian, I say thank you for the memories as well. You have enriched my life forever.

TV TIMEOUT—You may be wondering why I spent so much time talking about Brian. Well, maybe this will help you understand why: Brian touched the lives of so many people that his funeral service had to be held at our church instead of a funeral home. There was a line that extended from the church altar, out the door, through the parking lot, and into the street. Loudspeakers were set up outside of the church because even our enormous sanctuary with a balcony, which could hold roughly 550 people, could not seat everyone who came to pay their final respects. It was a testament to Brian and what he meant to our community.

Before I knew it, the 1997 season was almost over. For me, it was really a tale of two seasons, season A being before Brian's death and season B being after he had passed away. I remember how extremely long the season seemed to me that year. It was a constant grind, a continuous struggle to prepare myself for each practice, let alone each game. Heck, the games were the easy part. It was Monday through Friday that was dreaded by all.

At least on Saturdays, there was no Coach Oliver in my ear telling me to get everyone lined up correctly. There were no classes to attend or mandatory study hall sessions assigned. There was no ridiculous curfew on Saturdays so finally we could go out, converse with the rest of our fellow classmates, and see other things in Auburn besides the athletic complex, our dorm rooms, and our position coaches.

October 28, 1997

Dear Rob Pate,

I can't tell you how Proud I am of how well you are Playing down on the Plains. Pretty imPressive for a Pure freshman Player from these Parts. Particularly imPressive is your Propensity for denying the Post Pattern. KeeP Playing like this and you'll be Playing Pro ball in Pittsburgh or Phoenix or maybe even for the Carolina Panthers.

OK, enough already. I was just trying to "P" as much in this letter as you did on Arkansas Saturday. I can't believe you. I get "stage fright" trying to pee in public restrooms and here you are peeing in front of thousands of people. Just what are they teaching you down there anyway!!

On a more serious note I must confess that I am amazed at how much and how well you are playing down there. Keep up the good work. You're making us all proud back home (even those of us who bleed crimson). I hope you are doing well in school and do remember how important your education is now and will be later.

I meant to write you this letter way back in the summer and I'm sorry I never did. But here goes... I can't tell you how impressed I have been with how well you have handled your success through-out high school. Most people are impressed with your athletic achievements but I am more impressed with the class with which you always seemed to handle all the praise put on you. If I ever had a son my prayer would be that he would carry himself with the dig-nity and humility that you have displayed at school. What a testi-mony to the others that look up to you so much. I know this is kinda heady stuff but I thought you ought to know. I've had people over the years tell me they wished their kids would grow up to be like me so I know the sense of responsibility that comes with what I've written. I know you can handle it and it won't go to your head so I thought you should know. It's not the football player Rob that I love, it's just simply Rob I love. I'm praying for you.

your Proud Pastor,
Stacy (Reed)

> **TV TIMEOUT**— Stacy Reed was my youth pastor at Centercrest Baptist Church. All of the pee talk was because of something I did against Arkansas. I had to pee incredibly bad, but I didn't want to leave the field and miss any snaps, so I just peed on the sideline as my teammates circled around me. Oh, by the way, the game was nationally telecasted on ESPN2.

Yes, that season drug on incessantly as I struggled to remain the same type of player who had started the season. We continued to win games, but I had become physically fatigued and mentally exhausted. And with only Alabama remaining on the schedule, I just did not think I had it in me to play another game.

Yeah, right!

This was the one that I'd waited to play my entire life. *The Iron Bowl. State supremacy.* Braggin' rights for an entire year were at stake. It was Auburn versus Alabama at Jordan-Hare Stadium, where the Tigers were perfect against the Tide.

There is not a rivalry in college football that compares to the Iron Bowl. It's a game that divides households and shreds friendships. It has the power of completely halting a state, as all eyes turn to the *game of the year*. People who could care less about football feel compelled to pick a side and cheer for *someone* in this game. It's as though it's required by state legislation!

As the game rapidly approached, numerous reporters from all over the South assembled on the Plains to interview us and get our thoughts on such a significant game. They would ask questions about childhood memories from previous Iron Bowls, and boy, did I have some memories. I recalled Van Tiffin's 52-yard game-winning field goal, Bo over the top, the reverse to Lawyer Tillman, and 'Bama's perfect 1992 season, to name a few. My mind was loaded with images and scenes from Iron Bowls of the past, and finally, I was going to experience it all for myself.

This game is why you decide to go to Auburn or to Alabama. We came into the contest with an 8-2 record and heavily favored against 4-6 'Bama. I had always heard the cliché, "You can throw the records out when these two teams meet," and afterward I found it to be the truth. Iron Bowls have a way of becoming closer than sometimes they really should be. To play in the Iron Bowl is truly a privilege that no one on either side takes for granted. It's a game that brings out the best in everyone involved, and both teams play the game as if they're the 10-point underdog. You go into the contest knowing that it is going to be an all-out war. A battle for *pride*. There's mutual respect, yet an apparent bitterness that makes this rivalry the best in the land.

I didn't really know what to expect as I sat in my room at the Days Inn in Lanett, Alabama, pondering the game that night. The upperclassmen did their best to prepare us for what was about to take place, but there's just no way to explain to someone who has never participated in this game what to anticipate. All I knew was that I had played this game a trillion times in my head. I had dreamed of this moment my entire life. *Wow!* I was about to take the field for Auburn University in the 1997 Iron Bowl.

I remember the opening kickoff, standing on the sidelines looking across the field at Alabama. All of my life, I knew that I would play in this game, but I just always thought it would be for them. Instead, I was in orange and blue, and I was proud of it!

Around the stadium, the pompoms were shaking in unison and as intense as I'd ever seen. As the kicker approached the ball, the clash of "War Eagle!" and "Roll Tide!" cries was enough to send chills shooting down my spine. I knew at that moment why I pushed myself so hard my entire life. I also knew that it was all worth it! Win or lose, I was now part of something very special in the state of Alabama. Well, did I say win or *lose*? Losing was *not* an option if I wanted to face my friends back home in Birmingham for Thanksgiving and Christmas. A win was obviously *the* only option.

TV TIMEOUT—I attended my first ever Iron Bowl in 1996 at Legion Field in Birmingham as an Alabama recruit. I was permitted only two guests, so I took Phillip and Dana to the game with me. Naturally, we sat in the heart of the Alabama cheering section because we were at the game as their guests. I had already privately decided that I was going to commit to Auburn, but I waited so that Alabama would send me tickets to the game. Well, Dana was a huge Auburn fan, and when the Tigers jumped out to a quick lead, she cheered as if she were the athletic director of Auburn University.

(Watch out, Mr. Housel!) Embarrassed by the evil looks Phillip and I received, we told Dana to either bite her tongue or go sit in the Auburn section on the other end of the stadium. She chose the latter and stayed there the rest of the game. Instead of being waited on hand and foot by the 'Bama Belles and enjoying the best seats in the house, Dana thought the congestion of standing room only with Auburn people was a much better deal. And you know what? She was right! She embraced the spirit of Auburn that night and will carry it with her always.

My first Iron Bowl was a hard-fought, brutal war. Alabama led pretty much the entire game because of Shaun Alexander's determined running display and a defense that "contained" Dameyune. And when Alexander scampered down the right sideline for a touchdown, putting the Tide up 17-6 late in the third quarter, I thought we were going to lose.

But with sheer heart and determination that could only be mustered by the intensity of the Iron Bowl combined with arguably the most foolish offensive play call in Alabama Crimson Tide football history, we found ourselves with a chance to win the game. Only seconds remained as Jaret Holmes lined up to kick his way into the hearts of Auburn people and the nightmares of 'Bama fans. Down 17-15, Jaret booted the field goal that kept Alabama fans shaking their heads, contemplating when or if they would ever win in the confines of Jordan-Hare Stadium. 18-17! We had beaten the Crimson Tide!

After the game as we walked down Donahue Street, it was evident how much this game meant to the people of Auburn. Old men were crying their eyes out; women were pulling on us in every direction and passing out hugs and kisses; toilet paper was everywhere as families scrambled to Toomer's Corner to carry out an old and extraordinary Auburn tradition. I thought that I knew the importance and splendor of the Iron Bowl, but I was only kidding myself. I was just learning exactly what Auburn versus Alabama means.

With our win over the Tide, we were the SEC Western Division champions. We traveled to Atlanta to play Tennessee in the SEC championship game. In one of the most exciting games of my entire career, we lost to Peyton Manning and the Vols by one point, 30-29.

Our bowl invitation came from the Chick-fil-A Peach Bowl which we would play against the Clemson Tigers. We trekked back to the site of our disappointing championship game loss, but we won the Peach Bowl and ended the season with a record of 10-3. Finally, the exceptional, yet wearisome season was over.

I finished my freshman campaign by being named to the freshman All-SEC Team. I started eight of the 13 games and accumulated 50 tackles for the season. I learned an abundance of lessons, the first being how to deal with the length of a college football season.

Most of you have absolutely no idea what we go through as football players at a major program. Hidden behind the fight song, the media guides, sports talk radio, and tailgating, college football is a grueling job. But it's not a 9:00 a.m. to 5:00 p.m. job like most of the working world of corporate America struggles through. No, it's more like a 5:00 a.m. to 9:00 p.m. job when we tally our hours up. I think many times people forget that we actually go to class—some of us take the most difficult curriculums the university has to offer—or have to hold some

Jake Scott Tribble, Brian's son, and I kick back in my dorm room at Sewell Hall. *Courtesy of the author.*

ridiculous job on top of school and football. Sometimes, I believe even the coaches ignore the fact that we are students.

We players are always joking about the most amusing term that supposedly describes us: the *student-athlete*. Obviously, some ruling body contrived this nomenclature, although it really has nothing to do with college football in the SEC (well maybe, *maybe* Vanderbilt). Why do I say this? Because they always and quite emphatically put the word *student* before athlete every time. But that doesn't characterize college football players for who we really are. Although we would marvel at the opportunity to be students first, the competitiveness of the game and the pressure to win force us to be athletes first and students second every time. You know it. I know it. And it's a shame!

Now, you may be saying to yourself that football should come first. After all, that's why you are there! You're right. I would never have been financially able to attend Auburn University without a full athletic scholarship. (I could barely afford it with the scholarship.) But you are asking me to settle for a second-rate education at a first-rate institution all because an SEC championship or a win against Alabama is more important to you than a quality education for me. *Right?*

Maybe I've got it all wrong. Maybe, my performance on the playing field as an Auburn Tiger was more important than my schoolwork. Should I have spent more time with my eyes on game film and less time with my nose in a book studying? Well, I'll tell you what we are told as college football players. They say that just by being a football player at a major successful program, many doors will open for us regarding jobs. That still remains to be seen. But I can say this, without football-related activities dominating every day of my life for the past four years, my GPA would have been remarkably higher—guaranteed. And in contrast, if I hadn't taken one of the most challenging curriculums, perhaps my football skills would have been sharper, dramatically improving my play. Who knows? What I do know is that no "student-athlete" should be forced to make a choice between academics and athletics, but very sadly, many do. The two are extremely strenuous to juggle, and many drop the ball in one of these arenas. This is a part of college athletics that needs revamping so that all athletes can flourish both on the playing field and in the classroom. But my guess is things will only get worse!

Another item that thoroughly astounded me was the way in which some of my teammates reacted to instructions. For many, it was as if they had never been told what to do, where to be, or how to act their entire lives. Man, being late for a meeting or a practice scared me to death. Not only when I was a freshman, but throughout my four years. I never wanted to give my coaches any doubt about my dedication or to challenge their authority. But apparently, many guys on the squad thought that commands were intended for everyone but them. They were late for meetings, talked back to coaches, skipped curfew, and ignored mandatory study hall sessions. I couldn't believe that they had the gall to do it. But many did it and did it often.

What else took time to adjust to in that first year? How about learning to deal with the openness of cursing on the practice field? You have to remember some things about me to understand why that took some time to get used to. I was raised in a home in which cursing was not allowed, *period*. I played four years of high school football for a coach who never uttered a word of profanity or permitted his assistants or players to vocalize any vulgarity, *ever*. Well, things were a bit different here, to say the absolute least. I heard words fly from coaches' mouths that were nowhere to be found in my guarded vocabulary. Words that I was embarrassed just to hear, let alone shout at the top of my lungs for all of East Alabama to hear. Sometimes the cursing was exceedingly piercing because the words seemed to shatter the hopes of young men struggling to make an impression. And sometimes the cursing was so comical that it was the only thing that got us through practice.

Coach Oliver was notorious for some of the things he would say. He never cursed just because he enjoyed the sound of his own voice, like some of the coaches did. Conversely, he cursed to drive home a point and to make sure we never forgot the mistake we had just made. But his curse words never flowed together well, which always produced a chuckle from whomever the barrage was intended for. You know how there are certain curse words that just go together; just as peanut butter and jelly go hand in hand, some expletives usually are joined together in a particular combination. Well, for whatever reason, Coach Oliver would always rearrange these traditional phrases, creating his very own classics that were hilarious.

TV TIMEOUT—The next time you attend a college football game and you are completely bored to death, watch the players who come off of the field and are handed headsets. On the other end of the headset is a coach who is pretty ticked off that this player failed to do something that the team spent all week practicing. I promise that player you are watching is not listening to the game's broadcast, the news with Paul Harvey, or to Master P. No, the poor soul is being verbally assaulted. Coach Oliver did it to me on a regular basis, making me feel as if all 86,000 in Jordan-Hare Stadium saw my mistake *and* could hear our unpleasant conversation. But then he would spew out a line of curse words that made entirely no sense at all, causing me to smile, *relax*, and move on to the next play. Am I promoting cursing? Not in any way, shape, or form. But the overwhelming majority of coaches have always cursed, and many more to come will carry on the tradition. All I'm saying is that if you insist on a having a foul mouth, at least use your brain, like Coach Oliver, and change it up a little bit.

The final item that took a while to grasp was the building tension between some of the coaches—in particular, between Coach Bowden and Coach Oliver. It seemed almost as if we had *two* head coaches, and in reality we did—Coach Bowden was in charge of the offense, and Coach Oliver took care of the defense. Rarely did Coach Bowden even stroll over to our field to observe practice, and occasionally we even practiced in different locations (defense in Jordan-Hare Stadium, offense on the football practice fields). He stayed with the offense, Coach Oliver ran the defense, and things were phenomenally peaceful on the Plains...for a year.

CHAPTER 3

Flooded Plains

When I hear people talk about Rob, I hear about his unbeliev-able athletic skill. I hear about his hard work in the classroom and about his leadership on and off the field. People talk about his commitment to Jesus Christ and to his family. All of these things are true, but that's not what comes to mind when I think of Rob. I think about using the ladies restroom in Sewell Hall before Tiger Walk. We never lost when Rob and I peed with the ladies. I think of a guy who did whatever it took to make sure the Tigers' RAW defense was on the prowl. I think of a guy who is talented enough to play any position on the field and who was humble enough to play out of position to help his team. Rob is the perfect model for a college athlete. He comes ready to work and play with something inside that elevates him to a higher level than his opponents. He'll do whatever it takes to bust your ass; he's a warrior. I cherish every memory I have with Rob as a player, as a leader, and most importantly, as my friend.

Alex Lincoln
Teammate
Auburn LB No. 43
1998-2000

My sophomore season was one of turmoil and division under the leadership of Terry Bowden (top), who left midseason, and Bill Oliver (bottom), who tried to build us back into a team. *Top photo by AP/WWP; bottom photo courtesy of Auburn University.*

The 1998 season was painful for all who love Auburn University. Everything about it was absolutely awful and sickening for a team that had enormous expectations going into the season. We were green at virtually every position and had a callow attitude, believing that another trip to Atlanta and the SEC championship game was inevitable. *The problem?* We were young, dumb, and a lot worse than we ever imagined. And it didn't take long for all of the country to see how far the Auburn Tigers had fallen in just one year.

When the Virginia Cavaliers came rolling into Auburn to open the college football season on ESPN, we were full of confidence and eager to embark on another championship season. When the Cavs left that night, we were a divided, heartbroken, and stunned football team. We looked around the locker room at each other in search of answers. We had failed miserably in our opener, getting shut out 19-0.

And although we traveled to Oxford, Mississippi, the next week and blanked Ole Miss 17-0, running our record to 1-1, deep down we knew that we were not the Tigers of old. After consecutive home losses to LSU and Tennessee, we completely fell apart.

With our record now 1-3, we had a players-only team meeting in order to refocus and come together as a football team. It was definitely needed because each loss created enormous divisions between us all, most noticeably between the offense and the defense. Instead of the meeting uniting a team that was in disarray, it became a finger-pointing, name-calling fiasco that made me ashamed to be a part of my team that night.

The majority of blame was placed upon the shoulders of Ben Leard, our starting sophomore quarterback, who was doing his best given the fact that defensive linesmen were in his face like gnats on simple three-step drops, and our running game was last in the nation. Some guys on the team had a problem with the way Ben handled adversity on the field, and they explicitly verbalized their brutal opinions.

Specifically, I recall many players upset about Ben smiling whenever bad things happened to him on the field. For example, if he threw an interception or fumbled the ball, he would have a sly grin on his face when the cameras turned to him trotting off of the field. Seemed perfectly harmless to me. I mean, everyone deals with frustration in different ways, and who am I to say how it should be handled. Well, obviously my teammates saw it differently and raided Ben with their blunt, insulting comments.

I was in complete shock at what I saw taking place. Our starting quarterback, our appointed leader, was on trial by those who had given up on him. Many became so outraged at the indecency of it all that they simply got up and left. It truly wasn't fair. The attacks on Ben didn't stop with the players, because every talk radio program seemed to be aimed at getting Ben to transfer. Things got so incredibly bad that his mother couldn't even bear to come to our games because of the constant criticism from neighboring fans. Ben deserved better than that, yet he took all of the fault-finding in perfect stride. The way that he handled himself over the next three years was extraordinary, and he became a model leader to me. Webster's Dictionary defines the word *hero* as "one with great strength, one of nobility, one of good character." Congratulations, Ben, you are a hero!

I walked out of that farce of a meeting on the verge of tears because I knew how divided we really were. I had worked and pushed myself so hard. For what? For this? I didn't think we would win another game the rest of the season, and we really shouldn't have. We had self-destructed from within, and it spread like a cancer to the coaches and everyone involved with Auburn football.

Ben Leard became a successful leader on the field despite the doubts of some teammates and fans. *Courtesy of Auburn University.*

TV TIMEOUT—The opening sequence of events during our contest in Starkville, Mississippi, against the Mississippi State Bulldogs is the perfect example of the type of season Auburn football had in 1998. Mississippi State was penalized 15 yards before the game even began for unsportsmanlike conduct during pregame warmups. Because we were the receiving team, that all but guaranteed our offense would start the game with better than average field position. On the kickoff, our returner carried the ball just past the 30-yard line; however, Mississippi State was offsides. That's another Bulldog penalty that Coach Bowden decided to take, forcing them to rekick and pushing State back five yards more. On the second kick, our returner fumbled the ball, which was picked up by a Mississippi State player and returned for a touchdown. Instead of Auburn starting the game with tremendous field position, we started the game by handing State seven points. It was the third game in a row that our opponent scored a touchdown before our defense ever touched the field, and it foreshadowed the unraveling that was about to take place.

We continued to separate into factions, and Auburn University continued to suffer through one of the worst seasons in history. After a midseason debacle at the Swamp against the Florida Gators, our record stood at 1-5, and the snowball effect was about to reach new heights.

As a group of players, we knew that this season was unacceptable. We knew there was growing dissension among the

Auburn fans, and believe me, the pressure was felt by all. We knew something had to be done to energize our team and bring us back together again. But we never expected to lose the men for whom we all chose to play at Auburn University.

Now, I realize that I don't know everything involved with the resignation, firing, quitting, whatever you want to call it, of Coach Bowden. Many rumors surfaced, and legions of talk radio personalities and football "experts" conjured up their own versions of what all went down, but I do know two things about the entire ridiculous nightmare.

First, Coach Bowden did not deserve the treatment he received from Auburn. He came to Auburn, inherited an extremely difficult situation, was commanded to play by the rules (which to my knowledge he always did), and was *the* most successful coach in Auburn's long athletic history (Coach Bowden ranks third, behind D.M. Balliet and G.H. Harvey, who combined to coach five games in 1893, on the Auburn all-time coaching leaders list). But after one season removed from a Western Division title, Coach Bowden was ousted from a program that he had crowned with success. In my eyes, that was absurd!

Second, the manner in which we found out that Coach Bowden was gone was even more ludicrous than the decision to fire him. It was Friday night, just as we were preparing to leave Auburn for Lanett, for the next day's game. We always ate dinner at Sewell Hall, received our pregame speech from Coach Bowden in which he gave us the "six musts to win," and then we'd see a movie and go to bed.

But on this Friday night, things were far from customary. Instead of meeting in the cafeteria to eat like we normally did, we were told to wait in the team meeting room across the street at the athletic complex. We sat in there for about 30 minutes before guys began to get restless because we could sense things were out of the ordinary. Buddy Davidson, the assistant athletic director, was running around the complex like a chicken with his head cut off, and he kept telling us we'd be eating shortly every 10 minutes. Finally, after about 45 minutes of waiting, without an explanation and no coaches in sight, we decided to walk across the street and start eating.

But eating had to wait because we discovered the cafeteria's locked doors. Some people decided to wait outside, some returned to their dorm rooms, but most, including me, went to the game room to watch TV or play pool. It was in this room that we received the information, along with the entire nation, as ESPN reported that Coach Bowden was out as head coach of Auburn University. We found out that the man who offered us an education in exchange for football was gone through a TV report. Now, that was ridiculous!

Later that evening, after we were finally permitted to eat, Coach Bowden did come by to tell us that the report was indeed true. He told us that he had been forced out, he had to make some incredibly difficult decisions, and he first had to protect and provide for his immediate family. I felt sorry for the man because he struggled to contain his emotions as he wished us luck in life. To me, the situation was comparable to a death in the family. After all, we spent so much time together as a unit that we considered one another family. But after Coach Bowden's farewell remarks, that was it. He was gone, and I've never seen him since.

The torch was reluctantly passed to Coach Oliver to inherit this plagued team, search for positives in a negative situation, and somehow ignite a flame under a team whose fire had fizzled out long ago. Under the appalling circumstances, he did an outstanding job.

Things instantly changed with Coach Oliver calling all the shots. Practices were noticeably shorter because he was a big believer in getting the work done and getting off of the field. We sure didn't argue with that. He continued to be the defensive coordinator, but he also managed to spend a good portion of practice with the offense. In my opinion, Coach Oliver enjoyed putting together an offensive game plan much more than a defensive plan. He would always tell us how he was a much better offensive coordinator than a defensive coordinator. I had to see that to believe it, because the man was a defensive genius in my eyes. He told me once that on Fridays, after all the preparations for the week were over, he would peek at the other team's defense to see how he would attack them from an offensive standpoint.

One of the first things Coach Oliver decided to do as head coach was to change the normal seating order on the buses going to the games. This was an awfully simple alteration that spoke volumes to a team split in two. Many guys on the defense had a problem with the offense occupying the first bus, leading the parade, as the defense brought up the rear. The offense was first at everything we did as a team, and we began to resent being second at all events. Our offended feelings reached enormous heights as the offense struggled to score points all season long, but our defense was playing better than ever, ranked in the top five in the nation in overall defense. We felt we were doing our part to win football games while in our eyes the offense did their best to fumble away each contest. We felt that if someone had to be second, it should definitely be the offense! Believe me, when things are bad you search for reasons to bicker.

So what did Coach Oliver decide was fair? He took the starters from both the offense and defense and put us on the first bus together, and he rode on the bus with us. Coach

Bowden always rode in the state trooper escort car on the way to games. Coach Tuberville later reinstituted the offense in the first bus and defense in the second bus plan, and he rode with the offense, which was perfectly fine with us. But when Coach Oliver climbed up onto that bus with his players, that made us feel special and we loved him for it. You see, it doesn't take much for players to respect and love their leader; it just takes a bit of acknowledgment and genuine care and concern for the guys going to battle. Coach Oliver gave us that, and we played our hearts out for the man in our final games that year.

As things changed on the field, I also adjusted to the realities of life as a college football player on scholarship when I

Alex Lincoln, Josh Weldon, Whit Smith, Heath Evans, and me. These guys were my best friends and truly remarkable teammates. We didn't always agree on everything—as you can see— I am the only one without bleached hair. *Courtesy of the author.*

wasn't on the field. After my freshman year, I moved off campus and noticed that as the bills and expenses piled up, money, or lack thereof, became an issue. The majority of people have absolutely no idea how ridiculous most of our financial situations could be during our playing days.

There is an impression that there's just this magic fairy who appears and passes out money orders and personal checks whenever we get in a financial strain. People think that we are given money, cars, clothes, or whatever for our performances on the field. Well, let me set the record straight. Either the magic fairy who performs good deeds for successful football players slept while the defense was on the field when I was at Auburn or we don't get a dime from anyone! And the answer is...The $100 handshake is nonexistent at Auburn University, at least for No. 31.

But then again, I never went around looking for a freebie, or a handout, or anything of the sort. But, Lord knows, there were nights I could have used the extra money. I never thought it made much sense that at the end of a quarter I had to eat peanut butter and jelly sandwiches for dinner because I couldn't afford to go to the grocery store. I wonder if any of my coaches were forced to eat peanut butter and jelly. I believe we all know the answer to that. That's not right, and it should never happen. How an athlete at an SEC institution could go to bed hungry and unable to buy dinner is hard for me to fathom, but I did it on a regular basis.

"Well, you should have made a budget and followed it strictly," you may be saying. "That way you wouldn't run out of money by the end of a quarter!" Okay, fair enough. Let's see you make $1,350 last for three months. That's right, $1,350 was roughly our scholarship check, which was supposed to last us the entire quarter. Let's crunch some numbers together, shall we?

Balance: $1,350

Rent. My rent when I moved out of Sewell Hall and into a house with two other teammates (Whit Smith and Josh Weldon) was $600 a month. So over the course of one quarter (three months) with only that one scholarship check, that's $600 per person.

Balance: $750

Bills. I'll be hilariously conservative and say that my phone, cable, power, and water bills combined to be about $180 over the span of three months. Remember I'm dividing my bills by three because I had two roommates.

Balance: $570

Gas. We'll say that I filled my tank up only 10 times in three months, which is obviously not the case, but will further prove my point, at $15 a pop. That tallies up to be another $150.

Balance: $420

Miscellaneous. Oh, by the way, have you noticed I haven't eaten yet and I'm already down to $420? Haircuts, Wal-Mart necessities, car maintenance, and school supplies—we'll just not even add any of this in our budget, because obviously the NCAA doesn't take this into consideration either.

Balance: $420

Food. Finally, let's eat! For three months, I've got $420. That comes out to $140 a month, and even further divided, $35 a week. That's garbage. And for two years, garbage is what I ate because that's all $35 a week will buy you.

Balance: $0

There was no eating out. No ordering pizza. No going to see a movie. No nothing. I had no money in my pocket, ever. And why? Just where does all of that money go? Who are the people that are sitting back getting rich off of my back?

In 2003, Auburn University charged $40 to watch a football game in Jordan-Hare Stadium. With 86,063 seats, that's $3,442,520 per home game. That's $3.5 million just in ticket sales. This number has increased almost a million dollars in just three years. And we got badgered for needing new pants to practice in or sleeves to wear in the cold. Shoot, for two years under Coach Bowden, we didn't even have long socks to wear in cold weather games. We had to cut the feet out of one pair of socks and pull them up over our calves to make it appear as if we were wearing long socks! Then, we'd get cussed out by the equipment staff for ruining a pair of socks! Completely ridiculous and very sad.

We also were not allowed to work during the season, and if we did manage to get a summer job, we were watched with an eagle eye to make sure that we didn't make any more money than the *going rate*. We had to fill out roughly 10 forms and had about six different signatures from Auburn officials, and by the time the paperwork was completed, you had spent more time running around campus getting permission to work than you actually spent working. But then again, that's the way they want it, right? What's the problem? What is everyone afraid of?

Over the course of my career, I believe the question that I was asked more than any other from friends and fans alike was, "Do you think college football players should get paid?" You better believe college football players should get paid. We know the money is there; let's give some of it back to the players and help solve this problem together. You know, it was difficult to pull into the athletic complex on a daily basis and see the extravagant automobiles that everyone and their families associated with college athletics cruise around in when an oil change for my car was a tremendous blow to the budget. The proportion of what our coaches made compared to what we were forced to live on is absurd, and before long, players will resent it and demand a change.

The process makes zero sense. The coaches get rich, the schools get rich, yet the main attraction, the reason the fans fill the stadiums and arenas across the country, the players, don't see a dime of the billions rolling in. Right now, football players are really no different than thoroughbred racehorses. Think about it, a horse runs a grueling race, and for what in return? Some hay and oats and a stable to sleep while its owner reaps the harvest of the horse's labor. College athletes are no different than that horse, although at least the horse actually *interacts* with the beneficiary of his work.

TV TIMEOUT—In an interview on a Birmingham radio station that I just happened to hear, Coach Jackie Sherrill, the longtime head coach of the Mississippi State Bulldogs, was proclaiming the tremendous need to pay collegiate players; he stated that the NCAA donated $5 million to the disaster relief fund after September 11, 2001. I can't think of a more worthy cause to which to contribute, but the donation begs the question: If $5 million is just lying around the NCAA offices, why not distribute a fraction of it to the players who help generate the profit? Apparently, the NCAA has become a booming business, a business that in my opinion needs a firm check in place.

The standard of living for college athletes is absolutely absurd, and those who fight to keep it that way should lose sleep at night. The money is there to distribute to those who churn it out, so *distribute it*. Sure, it may be hard to do, figure it out! People always wonder why some athletes choose to accept money and other gifts illegally when offered. I'll tell you why. Because we're forced to live on nothing while others associated with our sports live in luxury. You show me the fairness in that!

On the field, our team seemed to respond extraordinarily well in our final games under Coach Oliver. He made us competitive again because guys seemed to raise their play to another level for him. We loved him for many reasons, but above all, we loved him because we knew he loved us. He was hard on us, yet he was a friend. He'd cuss you out when you screwed up, but he'd put his arm around you and tell you he loved you walking off of the practice field together. The bottom line was he treated us like grown men, and we respected him for that. And at the season's end, we began to push him as the players' choice for the permanent head coaching job.

TV TIMEOUT—In my two years with Coach Oliver, he would often tell me that I was a "breath of fresh air" because I was smart enough to run his defenses. Whenever he spoke to touchdown clubs, he loved to tell this story that he made up about me. He would say that I could sit at a railroad crossing as a train roared by and add the long numbers on each train car as they rushed by (390876, 567473, 985731, etc.). As soon as the last car passed, he said I could have the correct number tallied up, instantly. He would tell this fabricated story to explain how smart he thought I was on a football field. But sometimes being the smart guy had its downfalls! At practices, whenever I messed up, he would scream across the field, "Damn it, Rob! I thought you were a Phi Beta Kappa!" In case you're wondering, that's the honor society, and unfortunately, I was not a member. Everyone always got a good laugh when he gave me that line. Well, everyone except me!

When Coach Oliver was interim head coach, I believe we all thought that he would eventually be named as permanent head coach at the season's end. After all, he was obviously capable, he was more than qualified, he was well respected, he was a proven winner, and he did a sensational job with a not so sensational football team. Privately, I knew that he was going to be the next head football coach of the Auburn Tigers. How? Because of a conversation Coach Oliver had with Phillip before our game with Arkansas that year.

The summer before his senior year, Phillip was offered a scholarship by Coach Bowden at his football camp. In fact, he was the first verbal commitment of the 1999 recruiting class. With Coach Bowden's departure, there was a cloud of uncertainty hovering over Phillip's head because he didn't know whether a new coach would honor the scholarship Coach Bowden had offered. Coach Oliver ended that worry when he talked with Phillip in his office before the Arkansas game. He told Phillip that basically he just had to jump through a few hurdles for the athletic director, David Housel, and the job was his. He also assured Phillip that the scholarship offer was still intact.

It was clear to me that the job was Coach Oliver's for the remainder of the season. After all, he told Phillip that the job was his, and Dana was a Tigerette, a football hostess in the athletic department, where the buzz was that he would be named permanent head coach any day. But the night before we played

Alabama, something happened that told us there was a breakdown along the way.

That night, Coach Oliver called a team meeting after our movie in which we all thought he would tell us he had been named head coach. To our surprise, the meeting took an unanticipated turn. He began to tell us what a privilege and honor it was to coach us, how no team should have been forced to endure all that we did, and that he loved us more than we would ever know. It was obvious the man was hurt, he was angry, and he was dejected.

We lost to 'Bama, in the last Iron Bowl to be played at Legion Field, to end our dreadful season. I remember after the game, I did a postgame radio interview with Rod Bramblett of the Auburn Network. Right after my interview, Coach Oliver was to take my seat for postgame remarks. As I stood up and started to walk away, Coach Oliver took me by the arm, looked me in my eyes, and gave me a hug. No words were exchanged. No words were needed. There was a mutual friendship, a respect, and a loving bond that two years together had created. When I left Legion Field that night, I fully expected that our time together had come to an end. I was correct.

So what happened? Did Coach Oliver make an assumption that never should have been made? Did Phillip just dream the conversation before the Arkansas game? The answer to all of the above is a resounding *no*. The powers that be told Coach Oliver the job was his just four weeks prior to the Iron Bowl and the end of the season. Then, the powers that be took from Coach Oliver the position that they had just presented him. Why? I have no idea. But I do know that when Coach Oliver walked out the door no longer the coach of the Auburn Tigers, a bit of me left with him, and I never was the same type of player.

TV TIMEOUT—In an article written by Rob Watson, assistant sports editor of *The Auburn Plainsman*, in July 2000, Coach Oliver expressed his feelings in regard to this entire predicament. He stated how underappreciated he felt because of the way his whole situation was handled. "Nobody ever said thank you, not one single time. Matter of fact, I had to go tell the squad myself that Terry was gone. And when the thing was over, nobody said, 'thank you.' I felt like an old whore!"

To Coach Oliver, I say, "Thank you!" Thank you for opening my eyes and allowing me to see the game of football. Thank you for stepping into an appalling situation and making us believe that we could win. Thank you for being honest and fair, and a friend. You were a one-of-a-kind coach, and it deeply saddened me to see you get mistreated. You truly were the highlight of my Auburn career.

But the on-field reality was that we just weren't a very good football team in 1998. Defensively, we kept things close in virtually each game, but offensively, things just never clicked for us. We had a ridiculous number of injuries on that side of the ball, including *five* or *six* centers breaking bones in their feet. That season, it was a cursed position because whoever took the position ended with a screw in their foot. That single position characterized the 1998 football season at Auburn University. Damned, doomed, blighted, and cursed! But, thank God, the misery was over.

Most of Auburn's fans displayed tremendous loyalty in an extremely treacherous time when allegiance was, I'm sure, hard

to swallow some Saturdays. One Saturday, in particular, stood
out in my mind and always will. It was in a last-minute home
loss to Arkansas, our first SEC game under Coach Oliver and
our sixth loss of the season. Although we had come up short
once again, I recall the fans giving us a standing ovation as we
exited the playing field. Now, that's loyalty, that's devotion, and
that's allegiance! It made me proud once again of Auburn
because our fans absorbed another wretched loss yet stood on
their feet and applauded our effort. You don't receive that type
of treatment at every school, but as I've said before, Auburn is
just different.

November 10, 1998

Dear Rob Pate,

*I am 13 years old and I will be playing football for my high
school, New Life Christian Academy, I am hoping I get to play
defensive end. I know you play safety so please don't think I thought
you play defensive end. You may not know our high school, but we
are one of the best, we hope we win the state title, we are 10-1 for
the season, this Friday is our championship game. Is it okay if I
could have an autographed picture of you? Thanks alot!*

Your fan,
Justin Wilson

We finished the season with a 3-8 record. We were 1-7 in
SEC contests with the lone win coming against the Ole Miss
Rebels. We were winless in SEC home games for the entire year.
It was truly a nightmare of a season. When I committed to
Auburn during the 1996 season, the people of Auburn were

enraged with another 8-4 lackluster season. I never in a million years thought things would get worse than 8-4 in my time at Auburn. All of the sudden, eight wins seemed like a national championship-caliber season. It was the most humbling of experiences for a group of young men trying to make the people of Auburn, our families, and ourselves proud.

TV TIMEOUT—Someone I really grew to admire in my time at Auburn was athletics director David Housel. I appreciated the fact that after every game I ever competed in as an Auburn Tiger, regardless of the outcome, standing at the locker room entrance was Mr. Housel, passing out high fives and congratulatory hugs for victories or a concise word of assurance and an acknowledgment of the effort we put forth even in losses.

I recall one afternoon receiving a phone call from Mr. Housel's secretary, in which she stated that he wanted to meet with Dana and me as soon as possible. We set up a time to meet the next day, but we had no clue as to what the athletic director wanted with us. What he said to us I'll never forget. He said that in all of his years watching, researching, and analyzing Auburn athletics, he had never seen anyone that represented the ideals and principles of Auburn University like I did, both on and off the playing field as well as in the classroom. Coming from a man who probably knows more about Auburn than any other, that's an enormous compliment.

Dana and me with Athletic Director David Housel. Love for Auburn literally radiates from him, and he was and still is incredibly kind to Dana and me. *Courtesy of the author.*

Personally, I had a notable, yet understandably overshadowed season at strong safety; I tallied 70 total tackles, two interceptions, and a couple of fumble recoveries, garnering me second-team All-Conference status in just my sophomore season. And Phillip, who had numerous scholarship offers, decided to bring his talents to Auburn and play college ball as a Tiger.

I would say the one and only true positive that comes out of a losing year is the break you get after the season is over. Although every team strives to play in a bowl game, a conference championship game, or ultimately the national championship, the season is incredibly long. While other students are spending Thanksgiving among family and friends, you, as a member of successful college football team, are hard at practice.

While they are enjoying the sights and sounds of the Christmas holidays at the local mall, you are enjoying the company of your strength and conditioning coach in the weight room. While they open their Christmas presents, you are away from home at the bowl site with no presents to open and no family to celebrate with. And finally, while they celebrate the beginning of a new year, you have 10:30 p.m. curfew as you prepare for your *reward*, a New Year's Day bowl game. If you are unfortunate and have a losing season, at least you receive a break and much needed time with your loved ones.

It always makes me laugh when I hear the mention of a playoff system for Division I college football. It seems that every year the idea gets tossed around because legions claim it to be the only "true" system that can fairly determine a national champion. Although true it may be, you show me an entire college football team that is willing and able to play three, four, or five more football games on top of an 11- or 12-game regular season, especially in a conference as loaded from top to bottom as the SEC. You're not going to find many. By the end of a season, most guys are held together by tape, braces, casts, and whatever else imaginative trainers can conjure up. Putting guys on the battlefield for more pounding and punishment, no matter how great the reward, is just not the answer. And judging from numerous conversations I've had with players all across the nation, I'm not the only one who feels this way.

TV TIMEOUT—If you research college football schedules from years past, you will discover that for decades the college football season consisted of 10 regular-season games followed by a bowl game. Over the past decade or so, the number of games

> played in a regular season has inconspicuously crept up to 12 games. Add on top of that a conference championship game and a bowl game, and you've got yourself a 14-game season for a highly successful team. If I were a record setter from an era gone by, I would be upset that today's players have three or four more games to accumulate numbers that I never had. I mean three or four more games a season for four years, and guys today play an entire season more than veteran players from not too long ago.

If time away from football is the reward for a losing season, then my teammates and I should have received a lifetime expulsion from the sport after the 1998 season. We had plenty to think about as the season came to a conclusion and an abundance of time to contemplate our future. Who would be our next head coach? Because Coach Oliver left, how many guys would quit, transfer, or turn professional? It wasn't long before we had answers to many of our questions.

Tommy Tuberville was named Auburn's 25th head coach on November 28, 1998, just one week after our loss in the Iron Bowl. "How did the players learn of their new leader?" you ask. Why, from a newscast, of course! I actually found out that Coach Tuberville was named our new head coach from Sheldon Haygood, a sports anchor for Fox 6 News in Birmingham, when he called my parents' home in Birmingham to get a reaction from me regarding the news.

Honestly, I was upset about the entire ordeal. I didn't choose to play at Auburn University under Tommy Tuberville. I chose Auburn because I wanted to play for Coach Bowden and

Coach Oliver. As a team, we felt betrayed and totally ignored. They left us in the dark throughout the entire season and then waited until we went home for Thanksgiving to make the announcement. We had no voice, no say-so, and no weight behind our words. This wasn't the Auburn we were promised. This wasn't the coaching staff we grew close to.

But college football does not shield you from the cruelties that life sometimes slaps you with. We were dealt a completely different deck of cards virtually overnight, and to cash in our chips and quit was not an option. There was nothing we could do but face the facts, go on playing the sport we loved to play, and do our best to adjust to circumstances that were entirely out of our control.

TV TIMEOUT—The first time I ever saw Coach Tuberville after he was named our new head coach was actually at a red light on campus the weekend after he was hired. Dana and I looked to our left, and there sat my new head coach in, of all cars for a man with a million-dollar contract, a baby blue Chevrolet Lumina. I remember Dana jokingly said, "I wonder how long he'll be driving that car?" Not for very long! The luxurious German import came rolling in by Monday.

CHAPTER 4

Winds
of Change

While coaching the outside linebackers, known to the Auburn football team as the rovers and whips, I had the opportunity to coach Rob Pate. Rob was not just a great football player for Auburn University, but he is one of the finest young men whom I have had the privilege to coach. He possesses the strength, speed, quickness, and enthusiasm it takes to play at a high level in the Southeastern Conference. But even more importantly is his knowledge of the game—he is one of the most intelligent players I have ever coached. Our players would echo the same sentiment. They looked to Rob for his leadership abilities and for his awareness and knowledge of our defensive schemes and game plan.

I can assure the Auburn faithful that there are great things ahead for Rob and his wonderful wife, Dana, as they raise their young family. I know that he has an extremely bright future, and I look forward to witnessing the great things he will accomplish.

Phillip Lolley
Defensive Backs Coach
Auburn University
1999-2003

Here I am sacking Michigan quarterback Drew Henson on the opening drive of the 2001 Florida Citrus Bowl. *Courtesy of Auburn University.*

It didn't take very long to realize that things were going to be quite different with a new coaching staff in command. As a matter of fact, it only took one workout before we all knew things had most definitely changed!

Coach Kevin Yoxall, our new strength and conditioning coach, put us through our first of many running sessions, aka *Yoxercise sessions*, just days after returning to campus. The entire team met in the indoor facility to run three *gassers*, as our new coaches watched quietly. A gasser is a 208-yard sprint in which you make four consecutive trips from one sideline to the other within a specific time limit, usually about 32 to 35 seconds for defensive backs. I, along with close to 100 of my fellow teammates, toed the line, eager to prove ourselves to a new group of coaches for the very first time. But unfortunately, the only thing we proved that night was that we had an uphill hike and an incredibly long way to go.

When the whistle blew for that first gasser, I recall guys running like I'd never seen them run before, trying to make a valuable first impression. Just about everyone made the required time, and almost everyone looked like they had no problems with the first gasser. Then the whistle blew again and we were off for gasser number two at a considerably slower pace. I remember sprinting through the line with two gassers now under my belt, feeling pretty good about things. Just one more left, and we were finished. But the final gasser got to me pretty good. When I made the turn for my last 50 yards, I had no control of my legs as I wobbled home just under the required time. Luckily, I had made all three gassers in time, but most of my teammates were not so fortunate. When I turned around to see how everyone was holding up, it became quite apparent that my condition was much better than those around me. We had guys throwing up all over the place. One guy was vomiting blood.

Another linebacker, Mark Brown, had passed out just as he crossed the line, falling headfirst at sprinter's speed into the padded wall right next to me. Some walk-ons decided then and there that football was not for them and walked out the door, never to return.

Yes, with our very first running session and encounter with the new coaching staff complete, our eyes were now open to the changes that were in store for the Auburn Tigers.

TV TIMEOUT—What makes this gasser story so amazing is that by the time my playing days were over, we could all run three gassers in our sleep without a problem. There were days with Coach Yox when we would run a dozen and think nothing of it. As a matter of fact, those three gassers on that first night was the least amount of running that we ever did for him.

Interestingly enough, in a conversation I had with Coach Yox prior to my senior season, we talked about that first night together. I asked him what he thought about us after our miserable initial performances. He said that immediately afterward, he went up to his office, turned the lights out, and sat with his head in his hands wondering what he had gotten himself into.

In my opinion, the finest action Coach Tuberville took upon his arrival to the Plains was his hiring of Coach Yoxall to run the strength and conditioning portion of his program. Although Yox was brutally cursed on a daily basis within the confines and privacy of the players' locker room for the ungodly workouts he put us through, we grew to love him like a father. He took a team that had become amazingly soft and out of shape and transformed us into leaner, stronger, faster versions of ourselves with a regimen so hard-core that he must have conferred with the devil in order to create it. After completing a workout for Yox, you felt as if you could survive the most daunting physical challenges that this world could ever possibly engulf you in. And after a few weeks under our new strength coach, we thought we had endured the worst. Sadly, we hadn't even scratched the surface!

The winter "off season" for most college football players across America is a hellish period. Winter usually carries with it an increased school load to compensate for the lighter load taken during the season. (By most players. I was never afforded this luxury thanks to my choice of curriculum.) Winter also ushers in *mat drills*, the ultimate ball-buster, three days a week.

Mat drills were a new entity with the arrival of the new coaching staff. During the winter between the 1997 and 1998 seasons, we did not have mat drills because, we were told, Coach Oliver didn't believe in them, and he convinced Coach Bowden to scratch them from the calendar. (Mat drills were replaced with speed work and agility drills coordinated by Auburn track coach Ralph Spry.) Rejoice! Rejoice! And again I say rejoice!

We had no such luck during our first winter with Coach Tubs. I vividly recall our introduction to mat drills on a frigid February morning before the sun had risen. We walked into the indoor turf facility absolutely clueless as to what we had gotten ourselves into.

We were met at the door by one of Coach Yox's GAs (graduate assistants) who instructed us to proceed to the closest wall. That wall contained a strip of tape for every person on the football team with his name and a number written beside it. For example, my strip of tape read: Pate 2B. The 2B told me what group I would be participating with that particular morning. After searching the wall for our names, we were informed to place the tape across our chest so that our coaches knew who we were. It was a very impersonal feeling, walking around a complex where I had practiced for two years and having to *identify* myself. I felt like a branded cow, grazing in the foreign field of a new owner. But I also understood the need for the coaches to know who was who, to get a feel for our faces, and to have an instant reference in the heat of a verbal lashing during our drills.

With identification correctly placed across our chests, we were told to line up across the field in rows of 20 so we could stretch. Looking around, I was trying to figure out what exactly would take place after the stretching was completed. There were bags lined up in one corner of the facility, cones strategically placed at other stations around the field, and coaches standing at these positions waiting to tear into us.

As soon as the stretching was over, Yox gathered us together to explain where each group would begin and the system of rotation. He then blew his whistle to start, and immediately, all *hell* broke loose. Coaches began yelling and cursing at us as though we had just harmed their families. The noise was deafening; you could not hear yourself think. They didn't discriminate, either, they didn't care who you were or what position you played. When you toed the bags, cones, or whatever apparatus the station required, you were going to be cussed out until the drill was completed. After about three to four minutes at that station, we would then "rotate," aka *sprint*, to the next station and do it all over again for a different coach. This proceeded nonstop for about an hour. As soon as all stations were completed, we lined up across the goal line to run 30-yard sprints. This was controlled by Coach Yox, who took his cue from Coach

Tubs. We ran sprints until either Coach Tuberville got tired, or it was time for him to take his oldest son, Tucker, who accompanied Coach Tubs most mornings, to school.

After all that, a humane person might call it a day, right? No, not the new and improved Auburn Tigers. We then broke off into our position groups and ran through some *real, useful* football drills—drills that were actually beneficial in the game of football in contrast to the hour spent on military training that we would never use.

Just because we were being pushed to our cardiovascular and emotional limits on the turf field doesn't mean that we stopped pushing weights in the weight room either. We were lifting four days a week, and it was probably more unmerciful than the mat drills.

All in all, that first winter was a wakeup call heard loud and clear by a stunned football team. We needed a severe kick in the backside, and it was promptly given. After a few weeks of it all, we grew callous and hard as if we didn't even notice what we were putting ourselves through on a daily basis. We just went out and got it done, and before we even realized it, we grew to appreciate the meaning of hard work. It was something we had amazingly, yet gradually forgotten in our complacency and apathy. An attitude began to develop among the ranks that hard work was the only way to rectify a team gone wrong. But it took some longer than others to accept this new attitude and agenda.

It was quite evident to me that the coaching change was a much easier transition for the younger guys to deal with. It was the older guys, the seniors and juniors, who just couldn't initially swallow the situation. The young guys had nothing else to compare the circumstances to. They were brand-new eager beavers ready to run through a brick wall in order to make an impression. For the guys who had been around the block a few

times, the "rule with an iron fist" mentality caught us completely off guard. Not that we didn't want to work hard or didn't
know how to work hard; we just hadn't been *forced* to toil to the
extent now required.

I can recall instances in the weight room before Yox and his
staff arrived in which an entire workout could be completed
without a coach ever seeing you actually lift a weight. Jerry
Fuqua (the strength and conditioning coach under Coach
Bowden) ran an honor system operation (which at the college
level should succeed, yet failed miserably) of which many took
advantage. During the season, we were allowed to filter into the
weight room at any point during the day that was convenient
for us, get checked off by Coach Fuqua or one of his GAs, and
complete a workout with virtually no supervision. Some guys
walked in, got checked off, and simply left.

Well, with Coach Yox, *every* repetition of *every* set of *every*
exercise was observed by his eagle eyes. He required us all to
dress exactly the same, Auburn-issued orange shorts and an
Auburn-issued gray T-shirt. He *assigned* us our workout times
and severely punished those who were even seconds late. He ran
a tight ship, and those of us who had been here for a while stood
bewildered, like a deer in headlights.

But over time, the severe workout routine became just that,
a habitual everyday occurrence that didn't even faze us. The real
complaining and the circumstances that caused the greatest
upheaval were the old guys having to learn new positions, an
entirely different offense and defense, and having to adjust to a
new position coach. That's when everyone's true colors surfaced.
That's when patience with a new coach and an open mind
toward his philosophy often took a back seat to pride. That's
when it was quite obvious who was going to buy into the system and who was going to turn a deaf ear to those now in com-

mand. And that's when the majority of the older guys chose the latter.

> **TV TIMEOUT**—"I am not your friend, I am your coach!" were defensive backs coach and defensive coordinator John Lovett's very first words in his inaugural address to his new defensive backs. "What a way to begin a relationship!" I thought to myself as I listened to my new coach's New York accent. Walking out of my initial meeting with John G. (as I used to call him behind his back—I have no idea why), I viewed a transfer to another institution inevitable. But over the course of my two years with my Yankee friend, Coach Lovett really began to grow on me.
>
> He was an incredibly—almost to the point of compulsive—repetitious man, and as a player who hated game-day surprises, I always appreciated a coach who covered all of his bases. And although I didn't always agree with what he preached, I did what he told me to do to the best of my ability. And by the end of my first year with the man, we had become friends even though he declared in our earliest encounter that he would not be my friend, just my coach.

In my opinion, the coaching change had no greater effect on any one player than it did on me. Why? Because I was forced to completely change my position. You see a quarterback under Coach Bowden still plays quarterback under Coach Tuberville, as does a linebacker, corner, running back, lineman, kicker, and

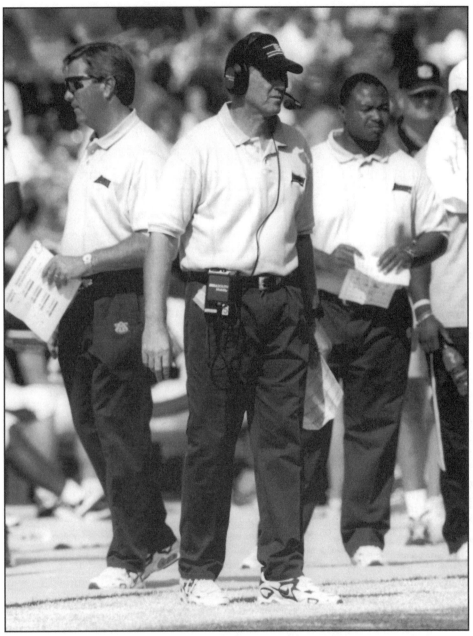

Coach John Lovett was our defensive coordinator for my junior and senior years. It was an adjustment to come off the field and face your coach as he cussed you out as opposed to the verbal bashing happening over a headset, which Coach Oliver did because he was in the box. *Courtesy of Auburn University.*

every other position—except a safety. My new position was called the *rover*, a hybrid outside linebacker. So as everyone else struggled to learn a new playbook, I also had to master a position that didn't even exist in our previous defense.

Also frustrating to me was that my mental responsibilities within the defensive scheme were nonexistent. Under Coach Oliver, I was the quarterback of the defense. It was up to me to get the call from the sideline, communicate it to my teammates, recognize the offensive formation, and get us into the correct coverage to fit our defensive front. It was tough, but it was right up my alley and played to my ultimate strength, my head. In my newly acquired role of the rover, my only mental assignment was to alert my teammates in the huddle where the ball was placed (either left hash mark, right hash mark, or in the middle of the field). Now there's a tough, mentally exhausting obligation!

Nothing about my new position of rover even remotely resembled my safety position of old. Not one thing! Instead of lining up 12 yards deep and back-pedaling on the snap of the ball, I now lined up directly on the line of scrimmage. Instead of being the unblocked eighth man to fill the hole of a running play, I became the blocking dummy for 265-pound fullbacks and 300-plus-pound pulling guards. *Lovely.*

Also very different for me was my role on the special teams. Under the old coaching staff, not many starters had to participate on the special teams because they believed in allowing the starters a much needed rest as well as making their backups earn their scholarships. Not so under Tubs. By our first game against Appalachian State, I was on the punt team, punt block team, and the kickoff team, as well as playing every defensive snap. I understood where the coaches were coming from, making the starters play special teams, but to look over at the sidelines and see 70 to 80 players dressed out when only 30 to 35 of us were actually playing disgusted me. At a program like Auburn University, I just couldn't believe that we had no one on the sideline who could take my place in the special teams department. But sadly, that was the case.

Off the field came the final challenging adjustment. I was becoming acclimated to my new role of husband. On July 17, 1999, in between our sophomore and junior years at Auburn, Dana and I were married at our church in Birmingham. What

Dana and me on our wedding day. Notice the Auburn football groom's cake. *Courtesy of the author.*

Several Auburn teammates at our wedding reception (from left to right): Jason Cook, T.J. Mears, Jeff Klein, Gabe Gross, Hart McGarry, Ben Leard, Courtney Rose, Phillip Pate, Jack Schwieger, Whit Smith, Josh Weldon, and Heath Evans. Seated: Antwoine Nolan, Ryan Hooker, me, Tellie Embrey, and Marcus Washington. *Courtesy of the author.*

a sensational thrill it was to call my junior high sweetheart my wife. I moved out of my house with Whit and Josh, and Dana and I moved into the smallest, oldest, most-wretched duplex of all time. However, we could not have been happier because we were eager to embark on our journey through life together as husband and wife.

But of everything previously mentioned, the position change, the lack of responsibility, the special teams assignments, the chore of learning a new defense, the differences in opinion and philosophy, and the challenge of being a newly married husband, all of that paled in comparison to the most torturous predicament I found myself in one night. It was a night that I will never forget, and one that changed my mental outlook on the game of football forever!

It was the first week of two-a-day practices under Coach Tuberville. The schedule was absolutely grueling, no different than any other two-a-day practices that I'd been through since junior high. After the second of our three-plus-hour practices, we lined up in the middle of the dusty, lumpy intramural fields—we held our two-a-day practice across the street at the intramural fields in order to save the grass on our own practice fields for the regular season—to run sprints. That particular night, in the heat and humidity of an absurdly scorching summer in southeast Alabama, Coach Yox decided we would run 40-yard sprints, two sets of six, within the specified time allotted.

Conditioning was never a problem for me. I usually won nine out of 10 sprints whenever we conditioned no matter the length of the sprint or the people in my group. And this particular night was much the same (even though half the guys in my group had practiced maybe a quarter of the time I had). But as I crossed the line and began to slow down with my fourth sprint now under my belt, I felt sharp cramps shoot down both of my inner quadricep muscles. A sip of water was totally out of the question. (Water was taken completely off of the fields we conditioned on. They say thirst, a natural, normal bodily occurrence, is a sign of weakness. Of course, I'm using the same sarcasm our coaches use when making that statement.) And the trainers were spread out all over the field tending to others who had already cramped up. I had no choice but to finish the set.

I ran two more 40-yard sprints with cramps shooting throughout my quads, hamstrings, and hips. And in between sets, I worked up the courage to tell our head trainer Arnold Gamber what was going on. He immediately said, "Man, let's get you on over to the training room. You don't have anything to prove to anybody. We just don't need you cramping up out here on this field!"

With that, I was off to the training room on my own power ... for two steps. The cramps in my quads were so painful and so intense that I could not straighten my legs. Therefore, two female trainers were forced to carry me off of the field ... for two steps. There was no way two women were going to carry a 215-pound guy, now probably 240 pounds with all of the equipment and sweat-soaked gear, a half mile to the facility. Instead, they instructed another trainer over their radios to bring the van out onto the field to scoop me up on the way to the locker room. Good call, girls!

Upon the van's arrival, I could hear moans and screaming coming from the back of the van. When the back double doors were opened for me to enter, there sat three of my teammates (Whit Smith, Tim Carter, and Mark Brown) in more pain than I was in. I crawled in and was handed a milk jug of Gatorade to drink, and off we were to the training room, aka *M*A*S*H*, where the real nightmare unfolded.

I was one of the first of about 30 guys who cramped up that night to enter the training room. I was carried into the training room on the shoulders of trainers Carrie Rubertino and Bryan "Mad Dog" Matson and placed on a table. I lay back, propped up by my elbows, and began to observe my other teammates who seemed to be far worse off than I was. IV fluids were being pumped into veins for rehydration at an ungodly rate, like water shooting out of a spray gun. I started to feel guilty for even being in there with these guys. I mean, for the most part my cramps had subsided, and the rest of my teammates were out there still running sprints.

I continued to force-feed myself the jug of Gatorade as my quads were loaded with ice packs. But after about 10 minutes without cramps, I thought I was for sure out of the woods. I was still propping myself up with my elbows, and my knees were slightly bent in order to keep a stretch on my quadricep. My back began to bother me, so I asked one of the trainers if I could lie down and straighten my legs. She said go ahead, and I did. And at that instant, I thought I was on my way to see sweet Jesus.

As soon as I straightened my legs, my hamstrings locked up, then my quads, then my hips, and then my calves. Every single muscle in my lower extremities was in knots. Doctor Goodlett (the Savior) came running over to shoot my arm full of valium and to start an IV. On his first attempt, as soon as he got the needle into my upper forearm, a barrage of cramps caused me to yell at the top of my lungs, shooting the needle out of my arm and across the room. He proceeded quickly over to my other arm, instructing me to either relax and keep my mouth shut or the IV would not go in and I would just have to sit there and cramp until the oral liquids hit the spot. I quickly became calm.

After all was said and done, my veins swallowed five and a half bags of cold IV fluids. After about 20 to 30 minutes of cramping in every muscle, *including* muscles that seemed to be created by all of the nonsense, the IV did its job, and I was finally cramp free. Physically, I was fine, but mentally I was scarred forever.

This one incident did more damage to my psyche than anything ever has or probably ever will the rest of my life. It was a trauma physically, but a death mentally. My mentality (something I struggle with to this day) became such that every muscle spasm and fasciculation I had registered in my mind as a muscle cramp building to a crescendo that was going to leave me in this same dreaded predicament. After that ordeal, I never thought of myself as the same type of player. My attitude became "Just get through it!" instead of "Be the best," which was instilled in me by Tim Cole at age six. It died that very night in the training room.

TV TIMEOUT—In August 1995 during two-a-day practices prior to my junior season in high school, we had a heat-related incident that was absolutely hilarious. Matt Dennis, our starting cornerback, was complaining during drill work about how extremely thirsty he was. As we stood in the back of the line waiting our turn to do the next drill, Matt told Jeff Hickman, our other starting corner, and me that he was going to fake passing out so that the coaches would be forced to give him some water. We called B.S. and thought he was just pulling our leg, but when Matt stepped up for his rep, just as the whistle blew, Matt *perfectly* (as if he'd been practicing for this) fell limp to the ground.

Coach Riddle, who was watching the defensive backs go through our drills, walked over to Matt saying, "Matt Dennis, you *will* get up off of this ground!" Just as Coach Riddle began to lean over Matt to help get him to his feet, Matt broke into a series of convulsions. Jeff and I stood there in utter shock even though we knew he was faking; he looked like a pro. We didn't know whether to laugh or to be worried as he continued bouncing about the ground. Suddenly, Coach Riddle's stern, adamant voice turned to one of compassion and mercy. "Matt. Matt, buddy. Are you okay? Come on and let's go get you some water!" Bingo! The magic word had rolled exquisitely off of the head coach's tongue. Within seconds Matt had his mouth around the water hose. As Jeff and I looked over at Matt submerged in the grandeur of the moment, he looked up at us with a sly, guileful grin. The son of a gun had pulled it off.

The 1999 season was one of ups and downs, new faces and new beginnings, and a different style of play. We were a much more aggressive group of guys because the off-season torment created a fierce mentality. Not much was expected from a team in shambles, a team coming off of a 3-8 record, a team that had three different head coaches in a two-month span, and a team that had fallen apart from within. And to be perfectly honest, I don't believe we expected much from ourselves.

August 1999

Rob,

Hey, hope this finds you doing well. I know this is a busy time of year for both of us so I'll keep this fairly short. First of all, I'd like to thank you for sending the poster. It says an awful lot about you that I make mention of it in passing on the sideline at a game, and you get it back that quickly. I don't guess that should surprise me though, it's the way you've always been, and that kind of gets to the main reason for this. Funny thing about this is that I've started this particular letter several times over the last two years and have not finished it for any number of different reasons (procrastination the worst of the bunch!). There are things I wanted to make sure you knew when you went down that I never got around to saying.

The period of time that you were in [high] school was without a doubt the most fun I've had in my career and that was because of the kind of guys we had playing at the time. Guys like you, Jay, Jeff, Matt and all of them made it that way. You guys had fun because ya'll were crazy enough to love what we were doing, and willing to work hard to make yourselves and your team better. I don't know if we'll ever have a group dedicated enough to make that spring 6:00 a.m. workout again. You guys were something special and I hope you all know how much we appreciated the work you put in. Most of the others in that group are around and I get to brag on them a little bit in front of the current guys, and I guess what I wanted to do was make sure you understood what you've meant not only to your school and football team here, but to me personally.

I felt fortunate to have been associated with you for those six years. You were a great player, but that's only a small part of it. You, just like those others that came through with you, made me proud because of that willingness to give what it took to get ready. I don't believe that we've ever had a group do that better. That's leadership and ya'll had it in spades. In your case though it went deeper. You know when people ask about you, and brother they do, the most common remark I make about you is that we just let you play and tried not to screw you up with 'coaching.' I believe though that what happened, for me, while you were there was this. You and those guys you played with reminded me of the fun in the game and why we do it and for that I thank ya'll. You just have no idea of what you all left me with. I'm very thankful for the examples that group made. You guys were kind of a measuring stick for what we look for

Above: The victorious Tigers
run off the field after
Alabama's last-minute fumble
in the 1997 Iron Bowl, which
allowed kicker Jaret Holmes
to lead Auburn to its first SEC
championship game.

Above: I celebrate after my first
interception as a Tiger at Ole Miss
in 1998.

Photos courtesy of Auburn University

Left: I make a defensive check in the 1998 Ole Miss game.

Below: Tiger defense shuts down the run against LSU in 1998.

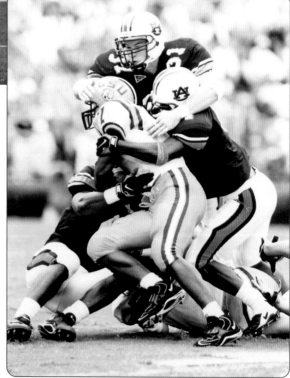

Above: I go in for a sack on Idaho's quarterback in 1999. I had five tackles, two sacks, two interceptions, a blocked punt, and an onside kick recovery in this game.

Below: Coach Tuberville questions me during the first quarter of the 1999 Iron Bowl. He called for a fake punt inside our 30-yard line, a pass that was intended for me. The pass was thrown low, and the play gave Alabama the ball. We held Alabama to a field goal, but he still grilled me about the play when I came off the field.

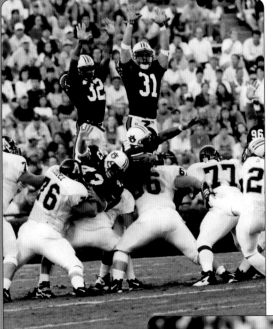

Left: Adlai Trone and I attempt to block a field goal.

Below: The Mississippi State Bulldogs were the most physical team in the SEC during my playing days.

Top: Even though I struggled during my senior season, I snuck up on Northern Illinois quarterback Chris Finlen in a nonconference game.

Bottom: We never doubted Coach Tuberville's intensity. Here he is with a big-time celebration for a big-time win.

My last interception as a Tiger in our 9-0 win over Alabama in 2000.

This interception was made in our end zone, ending Alabama's only scoring threat of the entire game.

Above: The Tiger defense celebrates a fumble recovery during the 2000 SEC championship game against the Florida Gators.

Below: Heath Evans and Alex Lincoln prayerfully embrace on the emblem of the 2001 Citrus Bowl. For both it was their final game as Auburn Tigers.

now, and you were the measuring stick individually. When I talk about success to these young guys I talk about a skinny little 7th grader who I nicknamed 'Spock' because I couldn't get him to speak to me or smile because he was so intent on playing. I talk about how he was the most talented guy in his class and how that wasn't enough for him because he had dreams of winning and playing better every week, and every year. You are still that measuring stick for me. I hope you understand that you taught as much as you learned with your spirit, your work ethic, and your faith. All of that you did leading that team kind of led me in a way too, and I appreciate it. Like I said, I've started this several times over the past couple of years and it's way overdue. I wanted to wait until some of the 'traffic' cleared over time. I know how much time and how many folks make requests and demands on your time because of who and where you are, and I figured I could wait until that traffic cleared a little.

By the way I didn't get a chance to congratulate you and your nuptials. I'm awfully sorry I wasn't there. We were actually probably passing you in an airport on the way back from Cozumel that weekend. Hope you had as good a time in Cancun as we did at Coz', of course you did, honeymoon!!!! Anyway, I guess what I've been trying to get across is that I'm proud of you 'Spock' for all the things you've become, and brother 'football player' is a long way down that list. Take care, have a great season, and come see an old fat man sometime.

See you soon,
Jeff (Estes)

As Appalachian State rapidly approached, the majority of our time was spent feeling sorry for ourselves. We sat and talked about how things used to be, how superior our old defense was, and how Coach Oliver would have never let this happen or that transpire. I guess more than anything it was just the only way we could rebel, the only way we could vent our frustrations.

No group of guys was more upset at losing their position coach than the defensive linemen were in losing Coach Pete Jenkins. They adored Coach Jenkins with every ounce of their being and rightfully so. He treated them like kings, and his deep compassion for each man he coached was evident in the tears that he would openly shed for them. It was this group that took the longest to buy into the new system. To Leonardo (Leo) Carson, Jimmy Brumbaugh, and Josh Weldon, it didn't matter if a reincarnated Vince Lombardi was Coach Tubs's choice as D-line coach; no one would ever replace Coach Jenkins. So when Coach Don "Sprint the Field!" Dunn came in and began teaching his new techniques, these guys went berserk.

I remember one incident in which Coach Lovett and Leo stood toe to toe ready to fight to the death at the end of one practice. During one of Coach Lovett's end of practice speeches, he made a comment that Leo took offense to. Instead of waiting until the meeting was over to confront Coach Lovett, Leo chose to deal with the matter then and there, for all to see. "When you speak to me, you *better* speak to me like a man!" Leo exclaimed right in the middle of the entire defense and all of its coaches. "I'll speak to you however I *damn* well please!" Coach Lovett asserted as Leo was up and in his face. The two exchanged unpleasantries face to face until Coach Terry Price broke the two apart. Afterward I realized that it was a good thing Leo had reacted when he did because if that meeting had taken place without Coach Price there to separate them, we would have probably lost our defensive coordinator (to death) and our All-America lineman (to prison). And although Leo should have never disrespected a coach like that, he just expressed the immense frustration and resentment that we all felt but were just too afraid to admit.

TV TIMEOUT—If the wisest decision Coach Tuberville made was to hire Yox as his strength and conditioning coach, a very close second was his decision to also hire Coach Phillip Lolley from North Jackson High School. Coach Lolley brought an upbeat intensity and excitement with him that only a coach coming from the high school level could bring. He had a passion for the intricacies of the game that became contagious to all. What set Coach Lolley apart from the other coaches was his willingness to stop and listen to what his players had to say, whatever the subject matter. His door was always open, and you knew that what you had said to him stayed with him. He was the definition of a players' coach, and I personally appreciated his caring style.

My frustration grew after Appalachian State for a couple of reasons. Number one was the fact that I felt like I should have just bought a ticket and watched the game from the stands. My new position as rover allowed me hardly any opportunities to make plays. All I could think about after the game was how extraordinarily hard I had worked for Coach Yox and for what? Two tackles! I was steamed to say the least. Second was the harsh reality that a last-minute touchdown was needed to win the game against a Division II opponent, an embarrassment in and of itself. I envisioned another season of doom and gloom, perhaps even worse than 3-8.

Coach Phillip Lolley and me after A-Day in 1999. Coach Lolley was unbelievable to play for and will continue to be a success at Auburn because of the mutual respect he and his players share. *Courtesy of the author.*

Just as I was ready to count us out, the second week against Idaho saw us make enormous strides in the right direction. Personally, I had a career game—five tackles, two interceptions, two sacks, and a blocked punt—and I recovered the onside kick to end Idaho's fourth-quarter threat. With the win, we were now 2-0 and on our way to Baton Rouge.

TV TIMEOUT—During my four years, I played against every school in the Southeastern Conference except Kentucky. And although no school's fans rolled out the red carpet upon our arrival, nothing could have ever prepared me for my first encounter with the nuts at LSU.

We both came into the contest ranked in the top 10 in the nation. It was a night game to be televised nationally on ESPN. I remember pulling into campus and seeing a line of purple-and-yellow dressed inebriated Cajuns stretching for miles down a straight road. They were all pointing us toward the stadium, as if they were directing us to our death. Small children, kids who couldn't have been more than seven years old, would make eye contact with you and then give you the finger. Then, as we cruised cautiously down the road, pants began to drop, one after another just as we would cross their location. The idiots were mooning us. And I don't mean just a few people; I mean entire platoons! It wasn't just the men, either. Women, kids, and heck, whole families joined in on the act. I believe I even saw a woman remove a baby's diaper to show us his butt.

And that was just the first wave. Second came the dousing of beer and liquor on our bus. This made it virtually impossible to see as we drove along. That made the rocks that pounded the side of the bus scarier because you couldn't see them coming. Although they were drunk, they were still pretty smart. And through all of this, the number of orange and blue T-shirts we saw could be counted on one hand.

That's because when we turned the corner of that dreaded street, the Cajun version of Vietnam's Street Without Joy or perhaps too much joy, there stood thousands of rabid Auburn nuts shaking their pom-poms in perfect unison to the beat of the band's drums. I was frozen with goose bumps that stretched from scalp to toe. It ranks as one of the top five visions of my Auburn career, and it was probably the best Tiger Walk that I ever experienced.

The 1999 LSU game is a funny story. Throughout the week, our tight ends and special teams coach, Coach Joe Pannunzio, declared the LSU game a "cigar game." In other words, a victory in Tiger Stadium meant cigars for all to be smoked on their field. Apparently, we were a team full of guys desperately craving nicotine, because we smoked LSU from the opening whistle, downing the Bengal Tigers 41-7. The game was fantastic, but after the game is when the festivities began.

Upon entering the locker room after the game, we were each handed a cigar by the equipment manager, Frank Cox. After our traditional singing of "War Eagle" and Coach Tubs's postgame congratulations, we all proceeded back onto the field and enjoyed our cigars on the LSU emblem at the 50-yard line. Sure, it was cruel. It was probably not the most humble thing to do. However, we weren't the first team to smoke cigars after a huge win, and we will not be the last. But what happened next was the most ridiculous occurrence in my playing days at Auburn and exhibits the astounding absurdity of the NCAA and other ruling bodies of college football.

The next week, Coach Tubs received a letter from the SEC's office in Birmingham condemning our actions in Baton Rouge. But what was so astonishing was that its gripe wasn't about the indecency or the improper ethics of what we had done, but rather the fact that we all broke the NCAA tobacco rule! This rule states that no student-athlete or coach is allowed to use tobacco products while participating in an NCAA-sanctioned event. Give me a break. If the courts hadn't banned the advertisement of tobacco products in the early 1990s, the NCAA would have every recognizable name in college athletics plastered on posters smoking away. *If* they thought it was profitable!

But the letter from the conference wasn't enough. Next came a letter from the NCAA inquiring how we *received* the cigars. Were the cigars a gift from the program? They deemed that we had violated NCAA rules, which I believe you can violate just by breathing, and in order to rectify the problem, we were all forced to pay Auburn one dollar for our cigars. Once again, the NCAA at its finest.

TV TIMEOUT—The NCAA has instituted many baseless, irrational rules of conduct. It is utterly mystifying. As an example, here is a circumstance that yours truly encountered as a recruit at Auburn University. My mother and I took an unofficial visit to Auburn my junior year in high school. We got the tour of the athletic facilities, met with some coaches, and spoke with a few players—you know, the basic visit activities. The director of football operations at that time was a super nice guy by the name of Bob Lacivita, and he accompanied my mom and me through the day's entirety, as we followed the schedule that he had created for my short trip. The last thing planned for me to do was to visit Jordan-Hare Stadium and walk out onto the field. This was when one of the most idiotic situations happened, which should have prompted me to start this book that very day. We had parked our car in the athletic department parking lot, and after visiting the stadium we were going to leave to return to Birmingham. As we climbed into our van, Mr. Lacivita said, "I'll meet you guys at the stadium." When we asked him why not just ride with us, he told us, "I wish I could, but that would be an NCAA violation." The football stadium was probably 300 yards from where our car was parked. So instead of just riding with us, Bob Lacivita jogged along the sidewalk, down Donahue Street, working to stay in front of us in order to direct us toward the stadium while my mom drove slightly behind him at about five miles per hour. It was a situation that made everyone feel awkward, and I'm sure pissed Bob Lacivita off royally. Only people with far too much time on their hands could have possibly created such a moronic rule.

Heath Evans smoking a cigar after our 41-7 victory over LSU in 1999. *Courtesy of the author.*

The win over LSU in Baton Rouge was crucial, because not only was it a victory over a Western Division rival, but also more importantly it was a new coach winning over the confidence and faith of his players. After that game, the old-timers on the squad finally gave Coach Tubs the approval and respect he deserved.

But just as Auburn football seemed to be back on track, five straight losses derailed our spirits as well as the belief we had placed in our coach.

October 7, 1999

Dear Rob,

We appreciate the effort you and our team put forth last Saturday in Knoxville. It looked like the defense came to play. You all are to be commended for hanging in there to the end. That effort is surely going to pay off—maybe this Saturday against Mississippi State.

I just want to encourage you to hang in there and never give up. Coach Jim Valvano wrote, "Don't give up. Don't ever give up." Whether you are on the football field, or facing life situations, down the road this will apply. We will see you at Tiger Walk Saturday.

A New Promise: II Chronicles 20:15

God Bless,
Wink (Chapman)

With back-to-back 3-8 seasons staring us directly in the face and with growing locker room disgust, one Friday night in a hotel meeting room in LaGrange, Georgia, changed everything.

Fridays before games were always a pretty chaotic time. We would always have a walk-through at the complex, board the buses at Sewell Hall, drive to the Ramada Inn in LaGrange, eat dinner (which was always fried chicken, lasagna, mashed potatoes, corn, salad, and cookies), have a short devotion, break into our offensive or defensive meetings to watch film and cover assignments, have a snack (which was always sandwiches and Gatorade), and finally sleep. Curfew was at 10:30 p.m., and yes, GAs came by to make sure we were in our rooms.

Well, on this particular Friday night, prior to our homecoming clash with the Central Florida Golden Knights, we added one more meeting to our already hectic schedule. But this was a much different sort of gathering. Instead of meeting to watch more film, to analyze our opponents, or to go over our critical responsibilities, Heath Evans, our starting fullback, decided we should assemble for prayer.

About two dozen guys voluntarily showed up for our first prayer meeting, which was held in the offensive meeting room. We circled the chairs around the small room as Heath read scriptures that spoke straight to the heart of our team. He then opened the floor for prayer requests or to anyone who had anything to say. We prayed for everything you can imagine—sick relatives and friends, traveling family members, the forgiveness of sin, no injuries during our games. You name it, and we prayed for it. After all the prayers were spoken, Chette Williams, our team chaplain, then ended the meeting with a powerful, moving prayer, as we all stood on our feet with our arms around our neighbors' shoulders. Upon the completion of Chette's prayer, we then broke off into our position groups based on whoever was there and prayed specifically for our position coaches. It was a simple action that created an amazing feeling of unity. And it was an action that for the next two years changed the soul of our team.

The next day, we beat Central Florida 28-10. It has been said that there is no such thing as an atheist on a battlefield; well, similarly, there is no replacement for a winning superstition in football. And though the prayer meeting was much, much more than a meaningless superstition, ending a five-game losing streak did wonders for our numbers at the next prayer meeting. And for the guys who hadn't experienced the power, the uniqueness, and the glory of God working in a football team the previous week, they came to see it firsthand the next.

TV TIMEOUT—Superstitions! Boy, did I see some crazy ones! Most guys will tell you that they don't have any superstitions, but they are lying if they do. It may have been as simple as getting your ankles taped by the same person every Saturday—I fell victim to this one; thank you Mike Roberts—or it may have been a certain routine you did each game day.

Cole Cubelic and Ben Leard used to put eye black on each other's eyes, whether it was a day game or night. Heath Evans always had to be the last man down Tiger Walk. Even the coaches were superstitious. There was a group of coaches and a few players who would drive to a restaurant in Opelika for lunch every Wednesday because they thought it brought us good fortune. I accompanied the group one Wednesday. We lost that Saturday, and I was immediately banned from stepping foot in the place ever again.

But probably the most outlandish of all superstitions was the one Alex Lincoln and I started our senior year and that he mentioned in his letter. For one game, we had to pee so unimaginably bad when we arrived at Sewell Hall for the start of Tiger Walk that we couldn't hold it until we got to the stadium. Apparently, we weren't alone. The line for the men's room was far too long for us to wait in, so we both stormed the women's room. (Mrs. Tuberville was on her way out as we walked in.) Because we won that night, Alex and I made peeing in the women's bathroom of Sewell Hall a pregame ritual. And you know what? We won every game at Jordan-Hare Stadium that year.

Attendance at the prayer meetings continued to grow over the last two weeks of the season. And as the room began to bulge with players and a handful of coaches, a bond began to form that was unbreakable. You began to realize how little you actually knew the guy in the chair next to you, the guy you've lined up next to for years. You began to realize that everyone has a story, that everyone has pain in his life, and that everyone needs encouragement.

It provided a shoulder to lean on in the midst of off-the-field turmoil that so many guys were experiencing. It allowed many the opportunity to come face to face with the demons in their lives that were holding them down. It was a time in which many of my teammates made the most important decisions in their lives, to accept Jesus Christ as their personal Lord and Savior.

And what those meetings did for us on the field was extraordinary. We were willing to lay down our lives and die for each other. We were ready to fight to the death for our coaches. Our level of play was noticeably more determined to win games for one another as we beat Central Florida and Georgia and took a much deeper Alabama team down to the wire.

The Iron Bowl in 1999 was hard to take. We were the first Auburn team to lose to Alabama in Jordan-Hare Stadium; however, Alabama was a tremendously talented football team in 1999, and we really outplayed them for three quarters. Missed opportunities in the kicking game, a back-breaking safety following a pivotal goal line stand by our defense, and Shaun Alexander owning the fourth quarter ended the steak. However, our effort proved to us that a team that prayed together jelled together.

Those prayer meetings carried over into my senior season and were the driving force behind our success. By the time we had our final nonmandatory prayer meeting, virtually every player and coach on the squad attended. The weekly prayer meeting had become just as important to us as film study or conditioning. It was a vital—no, it was *the* most essential meeting of the week. And of all the moments I've experienced as an Auburn Tiger, it's the prayer meetings that we had together that I'll treasure the most.

TV TIMEOUT—Over the course of my Auburn career, I've met people from all over the country who love Auburn football. But there's one boy in particular whose love of Auburn football caused a great awakening within my heart and forced me, as well as several of my teammates, to view football in a different light. Justin McBurney is his name, and since my junior year, we've been pals. Justin struggles with the everyday battles muscular dystrophy hurls his way, yet his attitude toward life is inspirational.

Justin could be found at every Tiger Walk sporting either his Rob Pate No. 31 jersey, his Cole Cubelic No. 61 jersey, or his Alex Lincoln No. 43 jersey. His face was always fixed with an enormous smile, and we all quickly grew to love him. We all embraced Justin as sort of a team mascot and always made sure we spoke whenever possible. And no matter how well we won or how badly we lost, Justin was always smiling and passing out hugs from his wheelchair. Justin McBurney's attitude was infectious to us all. He revealed to us how much Auburn football means to people, and he did it at a time in our careers when we needed it most.

Justin McBurney and me at Fan Day. Justin reminded us all of the importance and splendor of Auburn football. *Courtesy of the author.*

I finished my junior campaign with 59 tackles, five tackles for loss, three interceptions, two sacks, a blocked punt, and four deflected passes. I also finished that season with enormous respect for Coach Tubs even though I didn't appreciate all of the times he told us one thing and did another. For example, in a meeting in Coach Tuberville's office prior to spring training before my senior season, Tubs told me that I would see "very limited action" this spring because springs are for letting the younger guys learn the ropes. I then played every single defensive snap in the spring game! Considering the fact that I had played more minutes and started more games than most of my teammates combined, I was one pissed-off hombre. But it was hard to not revere a coach who took so many chances. Fake punts inside our own 20-yard line, fake field goals in which the holder tosses the ball *blindly* to the kicker, and onside kicks in the first quarter kept things interesting and fun, to say the least.

But I believe more than anything, I appreciated him for the direction of our program under his command. I applauded his willingness to allow our prayer meetings and admired his perfect attendance. I valued the work ethic he instilled in our team and the toughness that work ethic created. We truly were a changed team, physically, mentally, and spiritually.

CHAPTER 5

A Season Remembered

Most people who know me best would say that I'm one who typically wears my emotions on my sleeve while Rob has always been able to hide his emotions even when things are bad. He is the most mild-mannered person I have ever known. I can think of only four times in my life when I have ever seen him cry. He cried when a close family friend was tragically killed at our church. His wife, Dana, managed to get a couple of tears out of him on their wedding day. And when their little girl Claire was born, Rob cried. (There may have been other times that I cannot recall at this moment, but I can assure you that there aren't many more.) The other time I saw Rob cry will stick with me the rest of my life.

In the summer of 2000, before Rob's senior year at Auburn, he somehow contracted a mysterious illness that kept him on the sidelines all summer and for most of the fall preseason practices. He just didn't have any strength or stamina, and when he tried to do anything strenuous, he would cramp up all over his body. His future was up in the air, and doctors had no answers for him. No one knew how he would be able to perform once the season started. On August 30, 2000, the team left Sewell Hall for a hotel in LaGrange, Georgia, to prepare for the kickoff of the 2000 season against Wyoming the following day.

It was my first game, so I didn't have a clue what to expect. In the hotel that night, after the team meeting, defensive and offensive meetings, and position meetings, most of the players got together for a prayer meeting. We basically went around the room, took prayer requests, and prayed for each other. Then at the end, Chette Williams, the team chaplain, asked Rob to kneel in the center of the room. He then asked everyone to put a hand on Rob and bow his head. Chette then prayed a most inspirational prayer. He thanked God in advance for the work He was going to do in Rob's life on and off the field. Chette went on to thank God for bringing Rob to Auburn and thanked him for the leadership and the intangibles that he brought to our program. Once the prayer was over, there wasn't a dry eye in that room. Each player hugged Rob leaving the room that night, many

My dad and I stand under the goal post of Jordan-Hare Stadium after Auburn's overtime win against the Georgia Bulldogs. This was the last home game I played. *Courtesy of the author.*

*stopping to tell him how much he meant to them. I already knew that
Rob was a special person, but I realized that night how many others
he had touched as well. It also gave Rob an opportunity to see what
kind of impact he had made on the team in just three short years.*

Phillip Pate
Brother, High School and College Teammate
Auburn LB No. 58
1999-2001

My final season as an Auburn Tiger was a mixed bag. It
was physically exhausting because I struggled to get
over a summer illness; mentally challenging because I
was asked to change positions once again (from rover to whip);
spiritually uplifting because the prayer meetings became more
and more powerful; and emotionally draining because of the
excitement of being on the field with my brother for a quarter
(against Northern Illinois), the thrill of beating Alabama in
Tuscaloosa, the amazement of discovering I was going to be a
daddy, and the sad reality of seeing my playing days as a Tiger
gradually ending.

In an attempt to capture all of these feelings before they
became fading memories, I decided to keep a senior year journal. Initially, I was going to use my journal only as a reference,
but midway through the season I decided to put it all in print,
word for word, so that you could get inside my head. This is an
accurate account of my true emotions at those exact moments.

March 27, 2000

Today was the first day of spring football practice. I am
excited because I am entering my senior season, and this is my
last spring training. Coach Lovett moved me from my previous

The senior class of 2000. Not a single guy made an NFL roster following our final season, but this group led Auburn back to Atlanta as SEC Western Division champs. *Courtesy of Auburn University.*

position of rover to whip. It's pretty much the same thing, so I really don't mind. The focus of spring seems to be to revamp our defense, which lost a lot of seniors, especially on the defensive front. We practiced for a little over three hours in shorts and helmets as it was basically a learning day.

We are off tomorrow, except for pictures and meetings, and will resume practice Wednesday in shorts and helmets.

March 29, 2000

Today was the second day of practice and the last in shorts and helmets. We practiced for about three hours, and, of course, Coach Lovett held the defensive backs on the field for extra work after practice was over. By the time I got into the locker room, everyone else was gone except us DBs.

After practice, I tried to go get some Claritin for my sinuses from the team physician, Dr. Goodlett, but our head trainer, Arnold Gamber, told me I couldn't see him tonight, I'd have to wait until 6:00 a.m. tomorrow. I wanted to slap him in the face. I'll never understand why people try to make things so difficult here at Auburn. I felt like I was being treated like a freshman. Oh well, just one more year.

March 31, 2000

Well, today was our first day of pads, and for the most part, I thought we had a good day, at least defensively. When we went against the offense in different drills today, we did very well. I think Coach Tuberville thought that the offense would push us around today because they have more guys with experience, but it didn't happen that way, to his dismay. It seems like every time the offense pushes us around, Coach Tuberville thinks we had a great practice, but every time we push them around, he says we had a poor practice. Either way, I could really care less how he "thinks" we practice; we know when we've worked hard and have gotten better as a unit.

Tomorrow's our first scrimmage of spring, and I'm anxious to see how it goes. Supposedly, I'm not gonna see much action in the scrimmages this spring because I'm a senior—that is what Coach Tuberville told me—but we'll see how that unfolds. I'm pretty confident that I already know how it will, so I'll lace my cleats up tight tomorrow. Dana came and watched practice today for a little while with hundreds of others, and seeing her face always makes things better.

Oh, I finally got my Claritin after practice today. Dr. Goodlett found me and gave it to me because he's one of the few people in the entire athletic department who actually deeply cares and has concerns for us all. He's the best.

April 1, 2000

Today's practice was the longest practice I believe I've ever gone through. I mean, it's spring training, and we had guys cramping up after practice. We had a controlled scrimmage today with no tackling, so it looked like the offense had a better day, and they probably did. After practice Coach Lovett told me my concentration level hasn't been there thus far, and he needed me to be more of a leader. Also I slightly pulled my quad during practice. After practice, Coach Tuberville told us the next few weeks were going to be very physical and have a lot of contact. At the same time, he tells the media otherwise. Dana was there again today, and so were Mom and Dad, and Nanny and Papaw.

After practice, we all went out to eat at Country's Bar-b-que along with Phillip and Mark Pera, his roommate in Sewell Hall.

April 3, 2000

Today's practice was another long one for the Auburn Tigers. I was slowed a bit with my quad pull but went through the entire practice. There was severe weather across the state today and even a tornado warning, but we just practiced right through it. Coach Tuberville said we would continue to have more contact as we progress through spring. Kevin Greene was at practice today and spoke afterward. He played at Auburn in the early 1980s, played 15 years in the NFL, and is third all-time in sacks.

April 5, 2000

Well, today was the defense's best practice so far this spring. We pushed the offense around in basically every drill and team period today. It was fun seeing everyone get excited about doing great things. Even the coaches gave us a tiny bit of praise after practice. I thought Phillip did well today in the drills that I saw him participate in. I think all he needs is an honest chance, and he'll be fine.

Schoolwork is becoming a problem for me now because it has become second fiddle to football, not by choice but by affiliation. Today I left home at 7:50 a.m. and returned home at 10 p.m. What a long day!

After practice, Dana and I went to FCA, listened to Heath speak, and ate Papa John's pizza.

April 7, 2000

Well, today's practice was probably my favorite of spring, short and sweet. We didn't practice long today because tomorrow's our first major scrimmage of spring. Coach said that we're going to go 150 plays! That's gonna last forever.

After practice, Dana and I, along with her dad and brother, met Whit, Josh [Weldon], Heath, Alex, and Jeremy [Toungett] at Provino's for dinner. We wanted to eat well tonight for our long day tomorrow. It was fun being with them all, away from the athletic department for a change.

Dana was accepted into the education department today, so that was great news. I'm excited about what God's doing in our lives.

My brother, Phillip, lines up to cover a kick. Being able to play together was very special for us. *Courtesy of Auburn University.*

April 8, 2000

Today was our first real scrimmage of the spring, and for the most part I thought it went well. Defensively, we gave up some yardage on the ground, but we held tough when we had to. The offense only managed one field goal on us all day. I did some things well today, but there's always room for improvement. We're now at the halfway point in spring, and we really are so much further along now than we were this time last year. Our scrimmage consisted of six drives of at least eight plays. After the eight-play mark, we didn't get off the field until we stopped them.

Rudi Johnson looked good running the ball against us today. I think he could be the difference in us having a great season next year.

Whit's shoulder slid out of socket for the fifth time since we've been here, so he's through with spring practice. He'll go to Birmingham Monday for X-rays and possibly surgery.

April 10, 2000

Today's practice was a fairly easy one. We didn't have much contact because we are having an 80-play scrimmage tomorrow at the end of practice. I finally got over my quad pull, but I strained my tricep during punt drills before practice. Oh well, I guess I'm getting old and falling apart.

April 11, 2000

Today, we went to the stadium and scrimmaged. To say we dominated the offense today would be a major understatement. The backs gained a total of -23 yards against us. I believe if we continue to work hard, we are going to be a great team next season and surprise everyone. I thought Roshard Gilyard really practiced well today at free safety. Phillip is making a lot of progress and is really doing well.

April 14, 2000

Today, we went over to the stadium to practice because all of the high school coaches from across the state and Southeast were there for the coaching clinic. Basically, we did a lot of drills and hitting. I had a good practice today and so did Phillip. He popped someone in an inside drill, and I got excited and ran off of the sideline to jump on him. Tomorrow, we have another scrimmage. The offense will come out and try to prove something because we've been dominating them recently, and all of the coaches are on them. Either way, I don't care. Just have to go out and do my job. I'm really beginning to enjoy myself and have fun in practice. I feel like I'm getting better every day. Whit had surgery today on his shoulder in Birmingham by Dr. Andrews. Dana, aka "Danho," came and watched today, and I always enjoy that.

April 15, 2000

Today's scrimmage was simply the offense's day to shine. For the first time since Dameyune Craig and our days of the run and shoot, our offense did whatever they wanted to at will. They scored early and often and most definitely won the war today. They ran the ball; they threw it; they looked really good today. I was impressed mostly by Heath, who combines speed and size like no one I've ever seen. Defensively, we did some good things, but ultimately we gave up way too much to call it a "good" day. Phillip got the wind knocked out of him and went down midway through the scrimmage. He came back, though, and finished strong. We lost our best receiver midway through the scrimmage in Ronney Daniels—he sprained his MCL in his knee.

Afterward, Dana and I went out to eat with Phillip, Mom, and Dad at Niffer's, and we watched the NFL draft. Only three days left of spring! AMEN!

May 26, 2000

Well, we've just completed about our fourth week of "summer training." It's not technically summer because it's still spring quarter, but we get an early start.

Things have been interesting since the end of spring training, to say the least. This past week, we had a player shot by his wife in their car, we had two players shoot a gun into the air at Haley Center in a crowd, and we had two players kicked off of the team. First of all, TE Lorenzo Diamond was "accidentally" shot by his wife as they drove through campus. He was shot in the abdomen and is still recovering. Next, DB Brandon Reed and WR Deandre Green were arrested for discharging a firearm on campus as well as possession of an unregistered firearm. Deandre shot the weapon, and Brandon was the one charged with possession. On top of this, Brandon was kicked off of the team for stealing backup QB Daniel Cobb's credit card and charging up to $2,000 to the card. That same day, DE Derek Magwood was dismissed for stealing as well, supposedly from Quinton Reese, a former player.

Coach Tub called a team meeting, and he was pissed off. He basically said he was going to implement a "one strike and you're out" policy. I was happy because I'm sick of my teammates making Auburn, as well as myself, look ridiculous on a state and national level. It's so funny how fast news travels when you screw up, especially when you play at Auburn. People eat it up, and they categorize the entire team as rejects based upon the actions of a few. No one ever reports that I drove an hour and a half to speak to children in the middle of a busy week. No one ever hears the good things we do for our community and other communities around us. No, to make the top story on all the news channels, you have to be a nuisance and a troublemaker. It's sad, but that's just how it is. I'm glad Coach Tub got rid of those guys because I'm tired of being portrayed negatively, and you can't win with teammates you can't trust.

As far as the off-season conditioning and lifting goes, it's been tough. We run and lift five days a week, and it's extremely difficult, especially by the end of the week. We have taken another step though in our training, and it is going to pay off for us in the long run.

Oh yeah, my academic adviser from the athletic department left last week for a new job in Mobile. His name is Arthur Ogden. I helped him move, and he gave me his fish because they wouldn't have survived the trip. I named them Billy-O and John-G after my two position coaches.

July 29, 2000

I can't begin to tell you all that I've been through since the last time I wrote. I would have to say that I have been to an all-time low for me. All summer long, I have been battling illness. I have been through fever, diarrhea, extreme muscle spasms, blood work, an MRI, a session with a psychologist, numerous trips to Birmingham to see a neurologist, more blood work, a muscle-nerve conduction test, and a muscle biopsy. So far, all of my tests have looked great, and Dr. Goodlett has diagnosed me simply with irritable bowel syndrome. Each day I must take two Buspar pills and six Essential Electrolytes. I've been so very frustrated because it is getting close to football season, and I feel so far behind. I want to have a memorable senior season, but I feel like this all will haunt me throughout it. People try and tell me that it's just something that I'm bringing on myself through stress, but it just doesn't make sense to me. I want so badly to just put all of this behind me and move on, but it just keeps bringing me down.

I can't tell you how awesome Dana has been to me through all of this. She's missed so much class, has been to every doctor with me, and has had to do all of the chores around the house; she's just done it all for me. Hopefully, all of this will end for us soon. Agents have begun to send letters to represent me. I got my first letter from the NFL from the Chicago Bears. Hopefully, I can get better, have a memorable season here at Auburn, and move on but not forget it.

I finally got Coach Oliver's phone number and will call him shortly. In a recent article in the school newspaper, he said he felt like an "old whore" when he left Auburn because no one ever said thank you for what he did. I know he wasn't talking about his players, but I will call and say thanks. He has been the highlight of my time here at Auburn.

I got to go to SEC Media Days in Birmingham this past week. There were about 650 different reporters from all over the United States there. It was exciting and an honor to be there representing Auburn, my family, and my friends.

August 15, 2000

I'm laying here in bed at 10:30 p.m., and Dana is making me write in my book. We are in the middle of two-a-days, and before I know it, I'll be stretching and form-tackling for yet another practice. Practice has been good thus far. Everyone has had a great attitude, and we've gotten a lot done. I say we, but I haven't done much at all. I try to do what I can, but I wear down pretty quick because of this new medication. Dr.

Goodlett has me on Essential Electrolytes, Buspar, Levsinex, Anaspaz, and Dilantin. I look like the dope man walking around everywhere carrying all of my pills, but I'll do whatever it takes to get better.

The Birmingham News ran a huge article on me about being sick all summer. Interestingly enough, they went ahead and brilliantly diagnosed me with a stomach twitch. Dumbasses! If all else in my life fails, at least I know I could always be a sportswriter. The news went national as I just watched Fox Sports tell the nation on TV that I have a "stomach twitch."

I feel like I am getting better gradually, and hopefully I'll be 100 percent on August 31 for Wyoming. There's definitely more excitement flowing through my bones than I thought possible a few short days ago. Practices have not been all that tough. We go from 6:45 a.m. to 9:00 a.m. in the morning. We meet from 2:45 p.m. to 4:30 p.m. and then practice again from 4:45 p.m. to 7:00 p.m. We eat and then have more meetings from 8:15 p.m. to 10:15 p.m. I come home, go to sleep, and then do it all over again, and again, and again. That's two-a-days.

August 19, 2000

Well, things have been pretty hectic the last few days. We finally got moved into our new house. Dana, along with Mose and Papaw, did all the work. All I did was wake up one morning at 160 Crawford St. and went to sleep at 915 McKinley Ave.

Today ended two-a-days. It was very much a surprise because we had a practice scheduled for tonight, but they canceled it.

Today was also fan day. It was a lot of fun seeing all those people and how excited they get just to speak to you. It makes me realize why I work so hard and go through with things. It was weird being down on the court level where all of the seniors are designated. It just seems like yesterday I was doing all of this for the first time. I sat next to Ben, and we were the last to leave the Coliseum because the line was so long. I enjoyed myself and smiled more today than I have in a long time. So many people were deeply concerned about my health and well-being, and that was shocking to me. Well, it's not really shocking, but awesome that people who have never even met me were thinking and praying for me.

I ran into Coach Oliver yesterday morning and talked for about 15 minutes with him. He looked really good, and he too was concerned with my health. He invited us up to his house the Saturday after the Wyoming game to cook us a "slab of meat." Words can't express how much I miss him as my coach.

Well, we only have seven more practices until game one. I think we are going to beat the hell out of them beyond anyone's expectations. We will surprise a lot of people this year, no doubt. One of the magazines has us picked 55th in the nation, and that's absolutely ridiculous. We are not the greatest team in America or even in our conference, but we all want to win, period. Because of that, and that alone, we will, and we will do it often.

August 20, 2000

Well, tonight was absolutely horrible. I didn't make it through half of practice before I just couldn't go anymore. I'm so frustrated and so miserable out there. I don't feel like the coaches are taking my situation very seriously. If we played tomorrow, I might make it through 15 plays if I was lucky. I have four huge ulcers in my mouth, and I can barely talk. Can things possibly get any worse?

Phillip had to leave the practice field tonight because of cramps. I had to drive him home because he was unable to. It brought back some terrible memories from a year ago.

Doc increased my dosage on the Dilantin tonight. I know he must be so frustrated about all this. I can never thank him enough for all he's done for me. I just wish I could make it through one practice without getting unbearably tired, without the fear of cramping, and without spasms all over the place. I just wish things were normal. I wish I felt healthy.

I wish you felt healthy too! I can't begin to tell you how bad it hurts to see you so miserable. I pray for you day and night! I firmly believe God will heal you.

I love you,
your wife!

August 21, 2000

Today was another miserable day for me. I couldn't practice today because I had bad diarrhea. Doc put me on a new medicine, Protozone, an anti-inflammatory, to help me not tire out so quickly. I'm so frustrated with things that sometimes I feel like it would be best if I just hung up my cleats for good. I'm so miserable right now, and there seems to be no end in sight. I feel like everyone is getting frustrated with me. I don't believe anyone truly understands what I deal with on a daily basis. I wish it was as easy as people try and make it—"Just go out there and push through it"—but it's not.

We're 10 days away from game one of my senior season, and I feel like I need 10 months to get ready to play. I feel like Courtney [Rose] deserves to start and deserves to play because he's gone through every practice and has done a good job. Ben

Courtney Rose was my friend and backup throughout our time at Auburn. *Courtesy of the author.*

talked to me after practice, and Heath did before practice, and both said just do what's best for me. I wish I knew what was best for me.

August 22, 2000

Today we had the day off. All we had to do was work out. After workouts, I ran six half-gassers on my own to try and build a little endurance in my legs. It's getting close to game one, and I'm trying my best to get ready to play.

Today was the first day of school of my senior year. Where has time gone? I'm taking ecology, vertebrate biodiversity, and physics. May God be with me!

August 23, 2000

Today was the first time I was able to do pretty much the entire practice. I felt pretty good through most of the practice, except I was nauseated. Dr. Goodlett said I looked great and that I "passed the test." He was concerned because I told him before practice that I was going to push it. I'm just glad I felt halfway decent. Hopefully, I'll continue to progress in the right direction.

Practice started at 3:15 p.m. and ended at about 6:15 p.m. Coach said it was one of our best practices. Today, we began working on Wyoming's plays. I also got a letter from the Oakland Raiders today. Only one week 'til game one.

August 30, 2000

Well, tonight is one night that I will never forget as long as I live. We are in LaGrange, Georgia, at the Ramada Hotel, resting up before week one of my senior season.

I began today with a trip to Birmingham to see Dr. Shin Oh about my illness. He told me that he believes I have no real serious problem. He diagnosed me with possible benign cramp disorder and told me not to worry this season, just play. I walked out with a new confidence in myself and in my body. For the first time in a long time, I felt like I was my old self again. I heard what I needed to hear from the only person I truly believe knew what was going on with my body.

Dana and I drove back to Auburn for practice (walkthrough) at 3:00 p.m. At 6:00 p.m., we left for Georgia. When we got here, we ate dinner, and then Mike Kolen (Captain Krunch) gave the devotion. After that, we had defensive and offensive meetings, and then snack. Then, we had our team prayer meeting. About 30 guys met in the offensive meeting room for the first prayer meeting, which, by far, exceeded my expectations.

We circled up, took prayer requests, and then prayed for each request as a group. We had people praise God for newly born nephews, ask God for forgiveness of their sins, pray for traveling families; you name it, we prayed for it. As we went around the room, I wanted to speak up and ask my teammates to say a small prayer for me tonight before they went to sleep about my ordeal. But as requests were taken and prayers were spoken, I found myself holding my thoughts and my tongue.

Then, when it seemed like the meeting was on the verge of wrapping up, Kendall Simmons began to say something. He talked about the struggles he has endured with his ankles and how he thought he would never play again because of the pain. As he talked about his situation, I was astonished at how similar his was to mine. It was then he looked up and said, "Rob, we're here for you." He said things were gonna get better for me and that my teammates were behind me no matter what I did in life. Then, Heath asked Chette to pray for me. They placed a chair in the center of the circle for me to sit in and each person in that room laid their hands upon me. Chette prayed the most beautiful and inspiring prayer of healing that these ears of mine have ever heard. I couldn't help but to cry like a baby right there in the midst of my teammates and coaches. It was absolutely amazing to me.

After the prayer, each player gave me a big hug and a word of assurance, as tears rolled down my face. I felt a closeness to each one of them. The hugs culminated in a hug from Phillip, Whit, and Heath. I truly felt the love of my fellow teammates and most importantly the love of God in that room.

Afterward, Cole Cubelic asked me to stop by his room so he could give me something. It was a two-page letter he had written me saying that I have been a role model to him. He also expressed extremely deep concern and care about my health and well-being as Rob Pate the person, not Rob Pate the football player.

Tonight, I realized how blessed I am. Tonight, I realized what I mean to this team. Tonight, I realized what this team means to me. Tonight, I realized the power of God.

August 30, 2000

Rob,

There are a lot of things that I have wanted to tell you for a while, but for some reason, I didn't. When you signed here I had a big chip on my shoulder about you! That's just the way I was. I heard a lot of things about you and Erwin. I said some very negative things about you that I never should, and I'm sorry. I feel like we have gotten closer over this, our last two-a-days. I have wanted to be a better friend to you for a long time. I just had a lot of growing up to do. I basically wanted to write this and tell you that even though I don't know exactly what you're going through, I have a pretty good idea. It really hurts not being able to perform up to the best of your abilities because of something you can't control. I understand that! You have been a real inspiration to me over the last couple of weeks, I have really been motivated by you and your actions. I know how hard it is to imagine how important you are to the rest of us, but you are. You have been through a lot, and everybody knows you're not on the sideline milking some injury! You have played in more games than anyone on this team, don't forget that. I pray every day that the doctors figure this shit out. Whether you ever play football again, you would be one of my role models. You have a lot more going on, and I respect that about you as well. I have heard all kind of things, like you redshirting, not playing, whatever! I don't care, because I care most about Rob Pate the person. And I want the suffering you have been enduring to be over and done with. Someone of your stature does not deserve this. But I guess there is a reason for everything, and I know you will overcome it! I have enjoyed having you as a teammate and friend. Getting to know your parents, wife, and brother has been just as special. Your dad has been a lot of help to me, and I really look up to him for what he stands for and who he is. You have all of these great people in your corner, so don't ever give in. Your team is one of the best ever assembled. I'm sorry that I will not be out there on the field with you Thursday night. You have been such a good friend in supporting me through that B.S. as well, and I want to sincerely thank you. I just wanted to thank you and tell you how much you meant to me and many others on this team. We owe you a lot. Last year after the Alabama game, I thanked the seniors for what they had done for me; Marcus [Washington] taught us how to hustle, Leo [Carson] how to fight, Jimmy [Brumbaugh] how to overcome adversity, Q [Quinton Reese] how to party, Dirty [Antwoine Nolan] how to have fun, and most all of them for their work ethic. But I want to thank you for showing me how to be a better person. Thank you Rob!

Your friend,
Cole Cubelic #61

TV TIMEOUT— Cole Cubelic was our center as well as our strongest player on the entire squad. He was a fellow Birmingham boy who actually played at Homewood High School, an area rival of ours. I always gave him a hard time because in 1995 they won the state title, but they finished second to us for the area crown. In the most exciting high school game of my career, we overcame a 21-point deficit in the fourth quarter and beat Homewood 28-21 in overtime. I reminded Cole of this on a regular basis, and then he would promptly show me his fat ring, which read 5A STATE CHAMPIONS! Then we'd both shut up until we saw each other again.

September 7, 2000

Well, it's Thursday night, two days before game number two and hopefully win number two. This week has been a long, long week preparing to play Ole Miss.

Today, which is usually about a one-hour walk through, turned into about a two and a half-hour full-speed practice. I think that nerves have gotten to our coaching staff as they get ready to go back to Oxford for the first time since they left. I can't really blame them for wanting to win this one so bad. We have a chance to set the tone for the rest of this season. A win against a nationally ranked opponent (No. 17) on national TV (ESPN2) in a hostile environment could and should push us into the top 25. It could turn this program around. It's been a while since we won a big game, but I believe we can do it.

September 8, 2000

I'm sitting here on the airplane, minutes away from take off to Ole Miss. Finally, I made it to first class. I'm sitting next to Ben, and he's talking about his wedding (on June 16, 2001). We were originally supposed to fly into Tupelo, but bad weather is forcing us to land in Memphis. I think we are prepared, excited, and ready to play this game.

September 9, 2000

It's 2:30 p.m., and in 30 minutes, we load the buses to head to Oxford. We know it's gonna be hostile, but I believe we're ready for it. How do I feel? I'm excited, anxious, nervous, and just ready to play. I just hope I have the stamina to stay in through the entire game. I hope we show everyone watching that we are ready to return Auburn to success and dominance.

September 14, 2000

Dear Rob and Dana,

I know that you are going through a tough time right now regarding Rob's health. There are so many uncertainties right now that make things worse.

But there's one definite certainty we can hold on to—God is a faithful friend. Be confident that He is fully aware of what's going on and He will be with us no matter how confusing things seem to be. Look back over your lives and remind yourselves of how much He has always been there before.

Please know also that the Lord takes one valley experience and does something very exceptional through it all. Right now, the Spirit is working in your lives to accomplish a unique work of God, it may be some time later before we ever see it. This is how He worked in the lives of the biblical characters. Claim the promise that through the mess comes a blessing.

We love ya'll very much and He won't let us down. In time we will be able to understand more clearly what's really going on. Look for His revelation of spiritual maturity so you don't miss it!

Rob, I'm praying daily for what you shared with me—less frustration, and more energy. It may be a little while yet, but I believe with all my heart that this will come. As you surrender this to God more and more you will sense a renewal that only He can give.

The book, Tough Times Never Last, But Tough People Do, *is really good. Read it slow and meditate on the powerful truths that are in it.*

I can only promise you that the Lord is doing a good work in your life. Ya'll hold on to each other and the Lord!

See you Saturday in Auburn.

"My grace is sufficient for you, for power is perfected in weakness, for when I [Paul] am weak, then I [Paul] am strong." 2 Corinthians 12:9-10

Peace and grace,
Brother John [Smith]

September 15, 2000

Sitting here with Phillip at the Ramada Inn in LaGrange, about to go to sleep. We are 2-0 after our win over Ole Miss (35-27), and LSU is coming to town for game three. We are ranked 24th in the nation now, and there is a lot of excitement in Auburn. We had a great prayer meeting tonight, and I am so thankful and excited with what God is doing with our team.

September 17, 2000

Well, for the first time since November 1997 the Auburn Tigers won an SEC home game. It was exciting, and the stadium was electric as more people piled into Jordan-Hare Stadium than any time before to witness a football game. We beat LSU 34-17. In my time here at Auburn, I finished 3-1 against the Bengal Tigers. The break in the weather finally came, and I felt wonderful out there. I was able to fly around out there and have fun for the first time in a long while. I was on the cover of the program book and that was exciting. Phillip played his first plays at Auburn on the kickoff team.

This week, we play Northern Illinois here in Auburn.

September 29, 2000

It's been a while since my last entry. I'll get myself caught up.

Last week against Northern Illinois, we won 31-14. We came out and took a 24-0 lead at the half and then let them pull to within 10 before we scored our final TD.

This week, it's Vandy. I'm excited because we have a great chance of really separating ourselves from the rest of the West. They do some confusing things on offense, and they move a lot of guys around, but if we play our keys and play with intensity, we should be fine.

Things have been difficult for me off of the field this week. Ever since I got sick, I've just never really fully recovered. Because of that, when I get home from practice I'm completely exhausted. The last thing I feel like doing is studying, so all semester I haven't. Throw on top of that classes that I'm totally uninterested in and the feeling of being burned out with school, and the result is failure. I've been forced to drop my vertebrate biodiversity class and pick up some B.S. course, probably created just for football players. It will probably put me behind in my plans, but I really don't care.

I've worried about grades for three and a half years now. Not that I don't care about my grades any more; it's just I realize that this could be the last football season that I ever play, and I want to take it all in. I take in every practice, every meeting, bus ride, Tiger Walk, interview, prayer meeting—all of it. I just want to enjoy my time with my teammates for one last ride.

We've finally got this program headed in the right direction, and I'll remember "times like these" for many years to come. I don't want the scientific nomenclature of a white crappie ruining that.

Phillip and I were on the field together at the same time for the first time against Northern Illinois. He even made a tackle while we were out there. I hope our team comes out and plays with a lot of heart and desire because now we are getting into the meat of our schedule. So far though, so good! (4-0 overall, 2-0 SEC).

October 6, 2000

Sitting here in Tupelo, Mississippi, getting ready to go to bed before our big test tomorrow against Mississippi State. Because Phillip hurt his ankle in last week's win over Vandy (33-0), I have a new roommate, future QB Jason Campbell. We have an excellent opportunity to really distance ourselves from the rest of our conference tomorrow.

We are now the only undefeated team left in the SEC. We are ranked No. 13; State is No. 20, and the game will be played on national TV on CBS. State beat Florida pretty badly last week, and they were ranked No. 3 in the country.

I know we have the talent and the unity to beat these boys; it's just a matter of going out and performing. Hopefully, we will come away with win number six. Record: 5-0 overall, 3-0 SEC.

October 20, 2000

Well, it's been a while since my last entry, and a lot has happened since. I wish I could say I have great things to write about, but unfortunately that's not the case.

Against State, we got outplayed in the first half, and they took a 17-0 lead. In the second half, we did some good things but just couldn't move the ball on their aggressive defense. In the end, we took our first loss of the season on the road by a score of 17-10. Record: 5-1 overall, 3-1 SEC.

Last week, we traveled to Gainesville to play the Florida Gators. I thought we were well prepared, but the momentum just never left their side. After we botched a fake punt attempt on our first drive on our own 28-yard line, they took the ball and created a new highlight film. They easily scored on their first five possessions and took a 35-7 lead into the half. We played better "D" in the second half, but in the end, we had suffered our second defeat of the season. Final score: 38-7. Record: 5-2 overall, 3-2 SEC.

During the Florida game, I left in the beginning of the third quarter with stingers in my left shoulder and a sprained right ankle. The X-rays of both injuries were interesting. First of all, my ankle revealed an old injury that was at the root of my problem. On the inside of my ankle I do not have a ligament that separates the two bones that make up the ankle. Therefore, nothing is preventing me from rolling my ankle over. My shoulder was even more ridiculous. It revealed a half-dollar-sized calcium deposit resulting from a broken first rib that I believe I suffered my sophomore year of high school. Dr. Goodlett said it is very uncommon to see this injury in football players. He said it looked more like an injury from a car crash; he said NASCAR drivers commonly get this injury.

Either way, both have slowed me in practice this week as we prepare for 2-5 Louisiana Tech, but play this week I will. We have the chance to have a winning season and become bowl eligible with a win. Although we are shooting for far more than a six-win season, it would be nice to go ahead and get the monkey off of our backs.

Dana and my parents join me on the field for Senior Day before the Tigers face Arkansas. *Courtesy of the author.*

October 27, 2000

Sitting here in LaGrange, Georgia, in room 166 at 10:40 p.m. before the game with Arkansas.

Last week we beat Louisiana Tech 38-28, which runs our record now to 6-2 overall and 3-2 in the SEC.

We have a big opportunity ahead of us tomorrow against the Hogs. If we win, we sit alone atop of the Western Division, and if we lose, we sit alone at the bottom. We are ready to play. We had three great practices this week; we put the pads back on for the first time in about seven weeks.

I've had a long week because I haven't felt very well after the game against Louisiana Tech. I've felt like I'm relapsing a bit with all of the stuff from the summer. I've been having spasms in my legs all day, including as I write this entry. I just hope we come to play tomorrow and that my endurance level is high all day. Tomorrow is also Senior Day, so I'll come on the field with Dana and my parents. Only two more home games left ever.

November 3, 2000

It's November of my senior year. Only two games left on the schedule, and it's the two big ones, Georgia and 'Bama.

Last week, we beat Arkansas 21-19 to run our record now to 7-2 (4-2 SEC).

This week is the off week, so we can finally take a Saturday to sit back and relax. This week, we practiced Tuesday, Wednesday, and Thursday in full pads. We had three good practices as we focused on fundamentals and then looked at Georgia for about 45 minutes each day.

After the Thursday practice (yesterday), the young guys had about a 50-play scrimmage called the Turd Bowl. We gave Bret Eddins the MVT award (most valuable turd).

After the Turd Bowl, the eight- and nine-year-old Center Point Stallions scrimmaged, and we watched. It was kind of nostalgic seeing kids who were wearing the uniform of my hometown from the park where I learned how to play the game down at Auburn on our fields scrimmaging.

Anyway, the big news this week came out of Tuscaloosa, where the university decided to fire Coach Mike DuBose, effective at the end of the season. Isn't it amazing how quickly things change? This is the same coach who beat Auburn in Jordan-Hare Stadium for the first time ever and the same coach who won the SEC last season and was voted SEC coach of the year. The same coach who was given a three-year extension on his contract to remain coach of the Tide, to bring stability to the team, and to recruit the state's talent was axed on Monday. The thing that was so weird about the whole ordeal was the fact that if 'Bama wins the rest of their games against LSU, State, and us, then they will go to the SEC championship game. The timing of the whole thing is just ridiculous in my opinion. If they didn't play us, then I would be rooting for them to win the conference. How dumb would that look, to fire the coach who won the conference in consecutive years? That's football in this state, though. When the fans become upset and they want a change, then the big money people start acting and the coaching staff never has a chance.

The same thing happened here in 1998 with Coach Bowden, so I know what the players are feeling and going through. They say to each other to hell with the fans, to hell with the university, and to hell with the big money people; let's just go out and win for each other. It's in times like these that you begin to realize how little the general public knows what you go through as a student-athlete at a major program. You're the last one to know anything, you're the one kept in the dark until the last hours, and then you're the ones left to carry the weight of the program. You're the one who has to step on the football field in the midst of controversy to try to win. People don't think about player-coach relationships or injuries that take away All-America players. No, all they see is the win-loss column, and that's truly sad.

Football is a different game nowadays, and it seems the players and coaches are the only ones who realize it. Anybody can beat anyone on any given Saturday. Every school in America has great players. The Central Floridas and Louisiana Techs of college football are eventually going to have their day in the sun.

You see, a fan sees a name of a school on the schedule and immediately makes a judgment of that team based solely on a name and tradition. They don't watch game films of the opponents. They don't take into consideration that this team has all of its starters back on defense or maybe has a four-year starting QB returning. You see, we know that, and we know every game is capable of becoming a dogfight. And when it does become one, the fans are disheartened that their team, with such great tradition and obviously better players, can't put away a team that, in their opinion, should not even be on the same field.

Well, welcome to the new millennium of college football. The first thing you can do is throw old traditions out the window. To win in this era of football, an experienced, reliable QB and a fierce running game are absolute musts to be successful. If you don't believe me, ask the former head coach of the Crimson Tide or ABC's most Southern-sounding football analyst. They're both out of coaching because of it. Fans need to support their respective programs regardless of what happens. Fair-weathered fans are the absolute downfall of college football programs. This is supposed to be a game, full of enjoyment and excitement. Sure, football is a tough game full of trials and tribulations as well, but nowadays the majority of the trials are because of off-field circumstances.

Look, with the exception of Florida State's 28-year-old QB, we are a bunch of 17- to 21-year-old men doing our best to be great football players, students, boyfriends/husbands, and citizens. But college football has become a job to players that for the most part is no fun. If we give it our best shot, please don't boo us because our effort came up just shy of your enormous expectations. We did not mean to ruin your tailgating experience or your chance to brag to your fellow working cohorts.

For the most part, you don't even know who we are or what we do on a daily basis. You weren't there to see me play a conference game on the road the day after a close family friend was murdered in our church, and you didn't see the emotions I was going through. You couldn't see our coach's pain when his sons were born three months premature and struggled just to breathe. You couldn't see my muscles continually firing and locking up causing extreme fatigue and causing all aspects of my life, not only football, to suffer. These are just a tiny fraction of the things that I have seen or experienced.

Now, I don't say all of these things because I want someone to feel sorry for us, or for me, or anything like that. All I am saying is before you make a judgment of me, my teammate, or my coach, remember that football is not the only aspect of our lives. Believe it or not, we are involved in other things in our lives.

To see the players at 'Bama going through this ordeal brought back a lot of memories for me. And even though they are our bitter rivals, we are still a fraternity of brothers involved in the same grueling process known as *college football*. When I saw them so discouraged by the fans booing them and the embarrassment it seemed to have caused them, it really pissed me off more than anything.

And I'm not so naïve to think that we here at Auburn don't have a few fair-weather fans ourselves, but I can say this: In 1998, we were having an even more miserable season than Alabama. Our coach wasn't even allowed the opportunity to finish the season. Yet through all of the controversy, the finger-pointing, the blame game, and the bullshit, our fans never wavered and came out in masses to support the players in our final games. I didn't realize it then, but I do now. We really do have great fans for the most part here at Auburn. I can vividly remember losing to Arkansas at home in 1998 in the final minutes (our sixth loss of the season) but receiving a standing ovation as we left the field that day.

That's loyalty, and that's what those guys at 'Bama deserve. They gave Alabama fans a year to remember and to treasure last season. How quickly things change and people forget!

November 6, 2000

You know how sometimes you just feel like everything in your life is a little more important after you go through a shocking experience. Well, the last two days have been nothing shy of mind-boggling.

Yesterday, after coming home from practice, I found my wife lying asleep in our bed. Thinking nothing of it, I kissed her on her head and started toward the bathroom as she began to awaken. When I asked her if everything was okay, I could hear the lump in her throat as she rasped an answer that I did not expect. "I have some bad news," she said in a low voice. Fearing the absolute worst, I braced myself on the side of the bed as I tentatively asked, "How bad is the news?" She said, "I think I'm pregnant," and immediately began crying like never before. I was expecting to hear that someone was dead, and recalling past memories of when Brian was murdered, I was ready to hear the most brutal news. Then, to hear that I was going to be a father was absolutely stunning and breathtaking. I told Dana that I loved her, that everything would be okay, and that things happen for a reason. She calmed down pretty quickly when she saw my reaction was not what she had expected. I can't imagine the way she must have felt all day, wondering what I would say or do, wondering how and when her body would change, and wondering how and when she should spill the beans. She has got to be the toughest, most courageous person I know.

Today, the doctor confirmed that she definitely is pregnant. We came home and called our parents, our grandparents, our brothers, and our aunts and uncles. Everyone was excited and very supportive, and I thank God for that. Dana and I are both stunned but are very excited about the birth of this child. We know things happen for a reason and that we can do anything by putting God first in our lives and by sticking together. Can you believe we are going to be parents? I don't know the first thing about it, but I can't hardly wait to learn!

November 17, 2000

Never again will I step foot in Jordan-Hare Stadium to play a football game for the Auburn Tigers. My last home game was played before a sellout crowd of more than 86,000 people, and what a perfect way to end my career at home. The final was 29-26 in OT, and it was a game that I will never forget. Our record now stands at 8-2 (5-2 SEC) with only Alabama remaining on the schedule. We ended the season 7-0 at home, something not done since 1993.

I felt wonderful throughout the game, and my energy never wavered. I made my first interception of the year (the sixth of my career) in the fourth quarter, and we scored three points off the turnover. After trailing 13-0, we kicked a long field goal to make it 13-3 before halftime. The first play of the second half, Rudi ran it down to the two-yard line, and two plays later Ben hit Reggie Worthy for the TD to make it 13-10. We kicked two more field goals, Ronney D caught a TD pass, and we were up 23-13. They rallied late and sent the game into OT. They got the ball first, and we held them to a field goal. Then our offense took it to the one-yard line and had first and goal. The game ended perfectly when Ben scored the final TD on a quarterback sneak right in front of the Georgia fans to end our playing days forever in Jordan-Hare Stadium. I could not have dreamed a better conclusion to our careers at home. I was so glad to see Ben score the deciding TD against the team he grew up watching, especially after all he's been through for the university and the teammates that he never gave up on.

Whit and me in the lobby of the Sheraton Hotel in Birmingham before the 2000 Iron Bowl. *Courtesy of the author.*

And now it's the Iron Bowl. For the first time in about 100 years, an Auburn football team will travel into Tuscaloosa to take on the Tide. To win this game and end my career 9-2 with at least a share of the SEC Western Division title would be absolutely amazing. The environment is going to be hostile, but I think it is going to be perfect. This game means so much to so many people, but it pales in comparison to what it means to this group of seniors at Auburn University.

We won't be remembered as the most successful group that ever came through the Plains. We won't, by any means, be remembered as the most talented collection of seniors in memory. But despite all we've endured in our four or five years here, a win over Alabama in Tuscaloosa would establish our perennial legacy. We would be forever remembered as a group that never quit, that kept the faith, and that played perhaps above our heads, but most importantly we were the group that bridged the gap. After two consecutive miserable seasons for everyone who loves Auburn, this 2000 Auburn team and senior class could restore Auburn's pride and thrust this program back into the national spotlight. The thing is we can accomplish all of these things with one more victory against our bitter rival. Yet a loss against 3-7 'Bama could tarnish it all.

November 2000

Rob,

Wow! What a couple of years has it been for you! I just wanted to say thanks for all your hard work and your ability to never take a rep, no matter what we were doing, off. You've got some very special qualities that make you a man to always respect. Always keep in touch—I don't know that you and Dana will stray too far away, but let us know what is going on. Remember that the name

"Yox" is great for a boy or a girl (sell that to Dana). Good luck Saturday and beyond into the future. Thanks again and take care.

Sincerely,
Coach Yox

November 19, 2000

What a perfect ending to a far from perfect career. We took the most united, together team into Tuscaloosa and Bryant-Denny Stadium for Iron Bowl 2000 and came out winners. 9-0! A shutout!

And to put icing on top of the cake, Arkansas beat Mississippi State in OT! Western Division champions! No one ever believed it was possible. No one, except the players. I told everyone back in August that we had the chemistry to go to Atlanta and make a run at the prize, SEC champions. And here we are 9-2 (6-2 SEC) with the opportunity to be crowned champions.

The game was absolutely amazing, and I had so much fun all day long. My emotions were mixed as I got on the bus in Birmingham at the Sheraton to travel one last time to take on Alabama. Excited because it was the Iron Bowl, the greatest rivalry in all of football. Proud that we were in the position that we were in, 8-2 and a chance to claim a share of the Western Division title. Nervous, knowing it was going to be a defensive struggle on a cold and rainy day in an unfriendly college football atmosphere. Sad that this was it. This was my last shot at Alabama. This was my last Tiger Walk. This was the culmination of 17 years of football for me. Scared? Never, not in four years of college football. Ready, like never before.

Defensively, as the game progressed our confidence grew with each snap. We began to realize that this was going to be one of those special days where we were going to execute and win every battle within the war. We began to realize that they were not going to score on us. And as our offense moved the ball consistently yet struggled to cross the goal line, we began to realize we could not give an inch. The only drive that they really had was the opening drive of the game when they quickly marched to our 30-yard line, but on second down, I was lucky enough to be in the right place at the right time and picked off my second pass of the year (the seventh of my career). After we took their initial punch and they came away with nothing, they never seemed to counter with anything. When the final horn sounded and Iron Bowl 2000 was in the record books, defensively we had written our own chapter of textbook defense. 'Bama finished with 135 total yards.

I was so proud of our team. I can't imagine another team more deserving of all that we have accomplished this season. From the very beginning, we were a group of guys who could really care less about individual performances or personal success. All that we wanted was to come together as a team and win games for each other and for the fans who stuck with us through the absolute worst of times. Well, here we are now.

Twelve weeks after being picked 55th in the country, we are the SEC Western Division champs. We go to Atlanta in two weeks to play Florida for the championship. We are 9-2 and ranked up there with the nation's elite. Why? Because we gave God all the credit, glory, and honor for everything we accomplished. Because we grew close to each other on and off the field. Because we bridged the racial divide that exists in a world that tells us we are not supposed to be friends. Because we believed in each other and we bought into the system. Because we prayed together, cried together, laughed together, joked together. Because we became a *team* in every sense of the word. And that is why we are where we are at today.

November 28, 2000

This week has been exciting as we prepare for the SEC championship game in Atlanta against the Florida Gators. They are 9-2, and we are 9-2. They are coming off of a 30-7 loss to Florida State, and we are coming off of a 9-0 shutout of 'Bama. They whooped us 38-7 in October at the Swamp.

Since that game, we have truly grown up and matured as a defense and as a team. We have gotten better each week and defied the odds just to get to this game.

Auburn has not won an SEC championship since 1989. We can go down in the record books as one of Auburn's greatest teams of all time and as one of the SEC's most surprising teams of all time. We believe we can do it. No one in America, not even our classmates, friends, families, or most of the alumni, thinks we have a shot. Most have already booked their reservations for the Citrus Bowl in Orlando.

How I would love to ruin their travel plans. I want to stay in New Orleans. I want to play in the Sugar Bowl. How sweet that would be.

December 1, 2000

In 1992, my Little League football coach Tim Cole and I made our way down I-59 in Birmingham to Legion Field and the first ever SEC championship game. I was 13 years old and probably the biggest Alabama fan of all time. I watched in the final minutes of the rain-soaked, freezing cold game as Antonio Langham stepped in front of a Shane Matthews's pass and returned it for a TD to win the SEC.

I never in a million years thought that eight years later I would be playing in my second SEC championship game, especially for the Auburn Tigers. In 1997, I took the field for the

Western Division champ Auburn Tigers as a wide-eyed, nervous 18-year-old freshman. I was on the field as Peyton Manning hit Marcus Nash for a 73-yard TD pass, putting the Vols up 30-29 with about three minutes to play. As a matter of fact, I had Nash within my grasp on our sideline and just could not hang on. We lost that game by one single point, and I told myself that I was the reason we lost because I let him get by. I remember vividly, boarding the buses underneath the Georgia Dome and breaking down emotionally at the sight of my dad, first in line to see the exiting players. I thought that for sure I would have the opportunity to play in this game three more times and maybe even win the rest of them.

I was very naïve to think that, but being a freshman, I really did. I did not realize how extremely difficult this game was to get to. I didn't realize we would go 3-8 the next season. I didn't realize that we would lose our coaches and have to learn from new coaches. I didn't realize that we would have another losing season. You see, I didn't realize a lot of things. But I think more than anything, back in 1997 as a true freshman, I didn't really realize what I was playing for in this game.

As three years have passed, I have come to realize that people only remember winners. People only remember champions. We fell one point shy to Tennessee, but people never mention that we led 20-10 at the half. They never mention that we picked off Manning three times and had them on their heels. They never mention that we were double-digit underdogs. No, when people look back on the 1997 season and future fans research the game, all they'll see is Tennessee Volunteers, 1997 SEC Champs.

Today, as a senior from the state of Alabama who has played four years in the toughest conference in football, I realize what this one game means. I know what's at stake. I know that with a win, this team will go down in every record book as 2000 SEC Champions. And no one, no one can ever take that away from us.

In 1997, we didn't have a person on the team who knew what to expect when we stepped on that turf in the Georgia Dome. I hope that this team can learn from this group of seniors that has been here and lost. Don't have any regrets when you leave that field. This may be the last time you ever get this extraordinary opportunity. In 1997, I had this game literally within my grasp and it unfortunately slipped away. I've regretted it for three years. I won't regret anything that happens tomorrow, and I hope that every player and coach on this team can say the same.

December 5, 2000

Well, the championship game was a huge bust on our part. We did not do anything well the entire night. We fumbled on the first play of the game, and immediately the tone was set. We ended up losing to Florida 28-6 to finish 9-3 with only the bowl game left to play.

After the game was over, the representatives from the Citrus Bowl in Orlando gave us our official invitation to come and be a part of their bowl. Of course, we all wanted to go to the Sugar Bowl in New Orleans as champions of our conference, but I believe we all realize what a great bowl game the Citrus Bowl is. Michigan will be our opponent because they are 8-3 representing the Big Ten Conference.

It should be a fun experience playing in a New Year's Day bowl. It will be my last football game as an Auburn Tiger, and hopefully, we will end it with a win and a 10-win season. That would be a special ending to my career.

December 12, 2000

Today, we had meetings at 3:30 p.m. and then ran sprints after meetings. This was somewhat surprising because it was *dead day*, the day designated as a study day for final exams. It's the day that all of the students at Auburn hibernate into their study caves and classes are canceled. Well, the football team is not afforded this same luxury since we have to stay in shape, both mentally and physically, for the Citrus Bowl. Tomorrow, we meet at 9 a.m., have a short practice, and then I have to go home because I'm speaking at a church in Moody.

December 31, 2000

Well, tomorrow could very well be the last time that I ever put on the helmet and shoulder pads. Having played this game virtually all of my life, that seems like an impossibility. Only one more collegiate game. Only one more time will I don the No. 31 jersey I've come to appreciate. Only one more time I'll play in the orange and blue. This could be my final football game ever, and I think right now at this moment, I just realized it.

Coach Lolley just came over and shook my hand and told me, "Good luck, this is a big one for you!" I'll really miss him when I go. I'll miss a lot of things. I've had a multitude of memories in my four short years. I'll really miss my teammates more than anything though. They've really been a family away from home.

When I first arrived at Auburn in August 1997, I had no idea how much I'd grow up. I've always been a guy who was more mature than others my age and someone of good character, but my time at Auburn has allowed me to become a man. I've been through a lot, probably more than any one student-athlete should have to endure, but I managed by the grace of God. I've learned many valuable lessons during my tenure here.

Whit Smith, Josh Weldon, and I spend some time at Jimmy Buffet's Margaritaville during our trip to the Citrus Bowl. *Courtesy of the author.*

Now it's all down to one more moment. One last game to go out and use the abilities that God so graciously bestowed upon me. A New Year's Day clash with one of college football's most storied teams, the Michigan Wolverines. The outcome of this game is really of no concern to me as long as I can look myself in the mirror 25 years from now and know I laid it on the line.

I'll think about a lot of people tomorrow. I've been thinking about a lot of people all week long. Those who have helped me come this far who cannot be there, I will think of them. I will think about Brian Tribble, as I do every day of my life. Tim Cole, my Little League coach. My high school teammates (Jeff Hickman, Jay Sanders, Matt Dennis, Matt Rothe, Christopher Martin). Coach Riddle and the rest of my high school coaches. But I think more than anybody, I'll think of my family. My parents, who have never missed a single game. They'll never know how much that means to me. My brothers, who really molded me into the player I am today through yard football games growing up. My aunts, uncles, and grandparents who have supported me throughout my life. And finally, my wife; without her, I may have very well quit before this season ever began. I've truly got a lot to be thankful for, and I am.

You know, college football turned out to be nothing like I thought it would be. And as these last days have dwindled down to one more night as an Auburn Tiger, my attitude is really bittersweet. But I can tell you this: If I had the opportunity to do it all over again, I would do it in a heartbeat. Auburn has really grown on me in my final year, and I'm proud of my choice to attend this university. I know that I am a better person because of my time spent on the Plains, and I hope that Auburn is a better place because of me.

I'm proud of you and I love you.

No. 42
(Whit Smith)

January 1, 2001

Well, my collegiate playing days are officially over. I believe I have played my final football game ever. We lost today to Michigan 31-28 in the 55th annual Florida Citrus Bowl in Orlando.

Things didn't end like I wanted them to, but nonetheless it's over. I didn't even return to the field after halftime because of the cramps in my legs. Instead, I was forced to end my time at Auburn listening on the radio while my teammates scraped and clawed with Michigan.

It doesn't seem fair to me that after all this time and having endured so much, I had to end it like I did. I just have to keep telling myself that things happen for a reason. Why, in my senior year, did I come down with all of these medical problems? I don't know. It just doesn't seem real fair, because by most accounts, I have done things the right way. Not just in my days at Auburn, but really my entire life. All I wanted was to be able to finish my playing days on my own terms, but unfortunately this thing got the best of me on my final day.

But I know that God has a plan for my life. And over the next few weeks, I believe that the Lord will reveal His plan to me. All I hope for now is that my health is restored. I really played this entire season at three-fourths speed. I was always hesitant to give it my all because I never thought my body was up to the challenge. Here very shortly, I will become a father, and I don't want to go through life at three-fourths speed. I just want to feel normal again.

But even with all of my problems and with the disappointment of how my career ended, I am still very thankful. I'm thankful for the memories made on playing fields around the Southeastern Conference. I'm thankful for all the wonderful friends I've made because I chose Auburn. I'm thankful for the platform the Lord gave me to travel across the state speaking to church congregations. I'm thankful for my education.

I just wish I could have finished strong with the rest of my team. I felt great early in the game, but my last play was a touchdown run by Anthony Thomas as I cramped in both my calf and my hamstring. And that was it. Dr. Goodlett did all that he could do, but my body just quit on me.

I'm proud of the seniors, though. We've been to hell and back, but we stuck together, we united a team, and we were successful. We earned a lot of people's respect and even had many old alums claim us to be the best team they ever saw come through Auburn. That's saying a lot, and I'm proud of that. For a bunch of nobodies who were picked to finish next to last in the conference, we have come a long way. I'll never forget this team and especially this group of seniors. Although statistically this season was by far my worst, this was the most memorable and fun season of them all.

January 1, 2001

Rob,

I know I'm always giving you silly notes, and saying how sweet your ass is, but I'm gonna be serious with this one. My opinion of you has changed several times over the last three years. At first, you were just the starting All-SEC-caliber safety for Auburn. Then, you were the quiet, almost silent player that passed me in the locker room. Next, you became my teammate, my leader on the field, someone who made me pumped up, and who I looked to when I was in trouble. However, your final position is one you will always hold, being my friend. I love you and Dana.

Alex Lincoln #43

As you can see, a college football player's mind is filled with a plethora of varying emotions. Emotions ranging from the disgust of two-a-day practices, where the hot humid conditions can bring the strongest man to his knees, to the elation of standing toe to toe with an SEC opponent and winning; from the satisfaction of helping your team win, to the disappointment of letting your team down; from the thrill of running out of that tunnel into a sea of orange and blue, to the agony of walking off

Above: Coach Tuberville presents a watch to me at the Senior
Watch Banquet. Below: My grandparents and parents join Dana
and me for graduation. *Courtesy of the author.*

Above: Alex Lincoln and Heath Evans carry me on their shoulders at the Senior Watch Banquet. Below: President William Walker and me at the Presidential Graduation Luncheon. *Courtesy of the author.*

that same field having lost the battle that day; from the confusion and pain weighing down the heart of a teammate having just lost a loved one, to the comfort and unity created as team kneels together to pray for their brother; from the joy of living out your childhood dreams, to the realization that your playing days are no more.

That's college football! That's the ebb and flow that coincides with the game we love to play. Hopefully, you see that it's more than tailgating on a cool, crisp fall Saturday. It's more than the weekly pots to the best guesser at work. It's more than sports talk radio, ESPN, and coaching contracts.

At the heart of it all is the player. And it is the player who makes college football special and ensures the game's popularity and survival. It's his passion, his love of the game, and his respect for those who have come before him that make college football what it is. It's the tremendous pride that he takes when he pulls his jersey across his chest, becoming part of something much larger than himself. It's the straining sacrifices he makes off the field in order to be his absolute best on the field. It's the hours he spends daily with his strength coach pushing his body beyond limits his mind could possibly conceive. It's the sleepless nights he spends with his nose in a book studying for tomorrow's test after his grueling day of lifting weights, watching film, installing a game plan, and practicing that plan to perfection. It's dealing with injury or illness and being forced out of competition after months of agonizing training. It's meeting extraordinary people whom you would never have the opportunity to get to know without football. It's having the opportunity to use football for all of its worth as a platform to reach others spiritually. It's the satisfaction of watching your hard work culminate in a New Year's Day bowl game. That's the college football I know, and that's the college football I love.

My days as an Auburn Tiger truly were very special and fulfilling. I made friends I'll never forget and always keep in contact with. I played for a set of coaches I admired for their knowledge and dedication and then for a new set I admired for their tenacity and work ethic. I played for a multitude of fans who supported us just as much when we were losing as winning. I played for a school that I grew up hating only to fall in love with its traditions and atmosphere. I played in a state where college football reigns supreme, where people pack the stadium regardless of the opponent, and where that one game at the end of the season makes or breaks your entire year.

Auburn was an amazing place to experience college football. And although I did not always agree with or appreciate the cards Auburn dealt its players on occasion, I'll forever be grateful to a university that afforded me the opportunity to don the orange and blue and play out my dreams that began at age five in the streets of Center Point.

How long ago that seems! How special my time was! My experiences as an Auburn Tiger have forever changed my life!

TV TIMEOUT—ONE, TWO! ONE, TWO, THREE, FOUR.... War Eagle, fly down the field, ever to conquer, never to yield. War Eagle fearless and true, fight on you orange and blue. GO! GO! GO! On to vic'try, strike up the band, give 'em hell, give 'em hell, stand up and yell, HEY! War Eagle, win for Auburn, power of Dixie Land! HEY!

Our second Christmas with Claire McKinley Pate, 2002. *Courtesy of the author.*

AFTERWORD

June of 1996 was the beginning of the next five years of my life and a time that I will never forget. During those years, I was fortunate to be involved in two Western Division championship teams (1997 and 2000) and make some bonds that will never be broken. But I was also forced to realize that everything did not always work out as we may have hoped or dreamed. Although I did have a somewhat roller-coaster career, I would not change it for the world. It developed me into the person that I am today. Learning to take things in stride and one step at a time were only a few of the gravely important character traits that I adopted during my time on the Plains. I am constantly catching myself being jealous of the athletes who are at Auburn today. I did not realize how fortunate we were until my eligibility had expired.

As I referred to earlier, the friends I made are the most important aspect of my career at Auburn. Teammates like Rob Pate, Cole Cubelic, Alex Lincoln, Ryan Hooker, Rodney Crayton, Brent Mueller, Josh Weldon, Whit Smith, and Jeremy Toungett are only a few of the guys who come to mind. Not only were each of these men next to me on Saturdays in the fall, but also we stood side by side throughout the entire year. Saturday game days were merely the tip of the iceberg. We worked continuously from two-a-days in the pre-season, morning workouts in the winter, or "Yoxercising" in the summer. We experienced college, everything from classes to study hall to late-night feeding frenzies at the IHOP, together as well. We were each other's support system for everything, for both the good and the bad. Being able to mourn a loss or take a pat on the back from them gave us the ability to quickly recover from a tough game and also enjoy some achievements. But we certainly did not gloat

*for long because as you know, your friends will always keep you
humble with practical jokes and constant laughter at each other's
expense.*

*My time at Auburn was well spent, although every waking
moment was certainly not my favorite. I am sure many of you can
recall the 1998 season. That was unfortunately a point at which I
was miserable and despised Auburn University, the fans, teammates, and everyone who had severely criticized my family, my
playing ability, and me. It was during those several months that I
utilized the friendships I had developed—using each and every one
of them as shoulders to cry on and to vent frustration. That year I
truly found out what type of character I had and also learned what
support truly meant. Believe me, it was very hard to get booed off
the field in Jordan-Hare against UT and to have messages on my
voicemail and for people to think I was not deserving of playing
time in an Auburn uniform. But I quickly realized that for every
person I wanted to blame, hate, and question for my poor play, I
could only blame myself. After all, that is what a quarterback is
supposed to do. Once I began making adjustments to my attitude,
I wanted to take a positive role in what was becoming an embarrassing season for the Auburn football team. As hard as it was, I
would tutor Gabe Gross and Meiko Collier two to three times a
week in order to help them understand the game plan for the particular team we were facing. I do not know if that was good or bad,
because the more I met with the young guys, the more games we lost
and the worse they played. It was not done on purpose, I promise.*

*Following that season, I was given a rare second chance to play
football. I knew that if Bill Oliver were given the job as head coach,
I would be all but forced to transfer. So it should go without saying
that I was probably the happiest guy in the world when I heard that
Tommy Tuberville was coming from Ole Miss. To this day, it is very
hard for me to say very many positive things about Coach Oliver
other than that he was a great defensive coordinator. I was unable*

to have any questions answered as to why I was going to be "run off." Therefore, I was glad there were going to be new faces in the complex so that I could have a fresh start and reestablish myself. Coach Tuberville gave me the answer I had been searching for. And to this day I owe the next two years to him for giving me that one chance I was asking for. It had been more than three months since I was able to get a straight answer, and I had finally gotten one. It was not that I was going to be the starter; he told me I would be given the chance to play again. At that point I was elated to hear those words come from our head coach's mouth. I knew then I had a lot of work to do and a lot of minds to change as to whether I belonged, starting with all of my teammates.

Over the next two years I was able to not only win my starting job back, but also I was able to help lead Auburn to several victories, including a 9–0 shutout of Alabama in Tuscaloosa. I feel extremely confident that 1998 prepared me for not only the next two years but for the rest of my life as well. I do not think that I will face anything more difficult than that particular season. But the positives that have resulted from my five years at Auburn outweigh the negatives tenfold. It may seem that I have been solely focused on the bad experiences, but that could not be further from the truth. I truly love Auburn University and know that for the things that it taught me I owe it the world. The friendships, the experiences, the commitment, and dedication are only a few of the reasons that I am in debt to Auburn. Each and every day I wish that I could have had several more years to wear the orange and blue. To be able to continue to develop a place in my heart for the "loveliest village on the plains" will always be a priority. As I grow older and raise a family, I will certainly raise them with my experiences in mind. They will certainly be able to sing the fight song and scream "War Eagle!" at a very young age.

Like I said, I truly love Auburn University. Its athletes, students, and fans will always be special to me. I guarantee you that if you ask any former player, they can recall a time when they were losing a game and no Auburn fans had left the stadium—they were chanting, "It's great to be an Auburn Tiger!" As a former player, those are memories that will always be there about the fans. Most definitely, the friendships I was fortunate enough to develop had the greatest impact on my days at Auburn and continue to impact my life every day. There is no doubt; I would not have made it without their constant support and driving competitiveness. It is certainly an honor to be able to express my feelings about my alma mater and to walk you through some of the experiences (good/bad) while I was there.

But the greatest honor comes by way of having the opportunity to talk about a former teammate, friend, supporter, and idol. Rob Pate was definitely one of the most influential teammates I had the privilege of playing with. He was the quiet leader. Everything he did was by example, so you knew that when Rob spoke everyone needed to listen and do so very intently. Not only did he perform on the field like a leader, but also he did so off the field as well. Being a loving husband to his wonderful wife Dana, a respectful son, and nurturing brother are only a few of the traits that made Rob an all-around model. On many occasions he and I were mistaken for one another during Tiger Walk and in public. So the biggest compliment I think I could pay him and his family would be that I could only hope to be a fraction of the man that Rob Pate exemplified at Auburn and continues to do so today as a husband, father, and son.

Thank you, Rob, for giving me this opportunity! I love you brother!

Ben Leard
Teammate
Auburn QB No.14
1997-2000

EPILOGUE

Since my last collegiate football game in the 2001 Florida Citrus Bowl, my wife and I have traversed a gamut of life-altering experiences ranging from becoming parents to an amazing little girl, to having the opportunity to play football professionally in the National Football League for the San Diego Chargers, to entry into optometry school at the University of Alabama at Birmingham School of Optometry.

Auburn University has also endured arguably its most wretched national disgrace in the annals of the institution's long history. Their debacle of the coaching situation following the 2003 football season and being placed on probation by the Southern Association of Colleges and Schools has made newspaper headlines nationwide. Also the release of Coach Terry Bowden's "off-the-record" interview discussing payments made to former players surfaced in the fall of 2003 and became a hot topic.

My NFL Experience

I signed a one-year contract as a free agent in May 2001 to compete for a safety position with the San Diego Chargers. As I look back on all that happened before and during my time with the Chargers, I'm ashamed to admit that I ignored God's plan for my life by attempting to chase my own will—the chance to play in the NFL—and turning my back on what God had in store for me all along.

What do I mean by that? It all started with an ailment that went unresolved the summer before my senior year. (God speaking to me, "I'm not so sure about this NFL business.") As a side note, I failed nearly every single NFL team's physical based entirely on word of mouth and fear of taking a chance on the kid with an unknown plague without even going through an actual physical examination.

With Dana's delivery date in mid-July, it meant that if I did manage to get drafted or latch on to a team as a free agent, I would be forced to leave my wife and newborn daughter for training camp. (God speaking to me, "You need to be there for your family!") Once again, God's will unfolding, but I was holding steady to my own.

Opportunities to prove myself and my physical well-being never surfaced as invitations to the NFL combine and the Senior Bowl never came. (God speaking to me, "Hey, buddy, get a clue!") As a side note, I would bet I'm the only four-year starter at Alabama or Auburn who's missed out on an invitation to the Mobile Senior Bowl since the game's inception.

As draft day approached, I was physically in superb condition having spent January through April training vigorously in Atlanta. Despite the baggage that went along with my recent health history, there was still a handful of teams talking about potentially drafting me.

On the second day of the draft in the sixth round, the phone rang at my parents' home in Birmingham. The caller ID showed the phone call was from San Francisco. I answered and was greeted by someone from the 49ers' staff. He informed me that they just did not have enough picks to be able to draft me, but that if no one else drafted me that day, the 49ers would love to sign me as a free agent. When San Francisco's final pick in the seventh round approached, I thought to myself, "Let's see who this guy is that is going be drafted in my place."

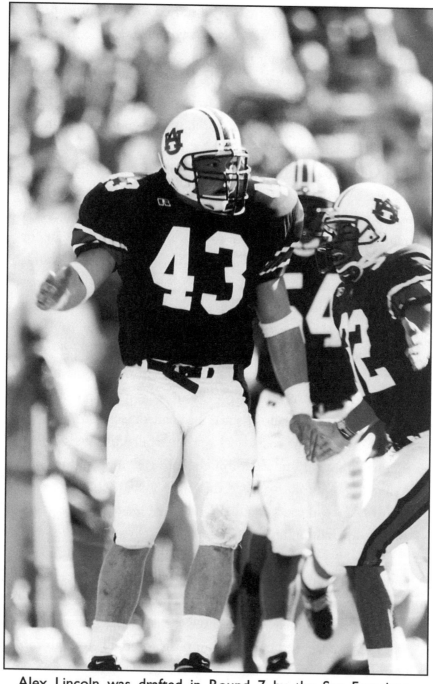

Alex Lincoln was drafted in Round 7 by the San Francisco 49ers. *Courtesy of Auburn University.*

"With their final pick in the seventh round, the San Francisco 49ers select ... Alex Lincoln, linebacker, Auburn University."

I lost seemingly my greatest chance to be drafted to one of my best friends. I never heard back from the 49ers after that.

Normally as soon as the second day of the draft is over, teams sign an overabundance of free agents that very night. As I sat and waited for the phone call to come that night, it never did, and the silence continued for two weeks after draft day. I had completely conceded to the reality that a shot at the next level was never coming and decided to take my wife to Florida to get away from all of the nonsense. We had just checked into our hotel and had gotten back from visiting the pool when a note on the door said there was an urgent need to get in contact with my parents. The San Diego Chargers wanted me at mini-camp the next morning. My NFL opportunity was all in order. (Rob saying to God, "I know what's best for my own life!")

San Diego had three returning safeties from the previous year, had drafted a safety in the seventh round from Clemson, had two safeties playing in NFL Europe, and brought in another free agent safety from Penn State. That would make a grand total of eight safeties competing for four or five slots on the final team roster. One of those safeties was an All-Pro performer, Rodney Harrison, and another was the Chargers' first draft choice of the previous year, Rogers Beckett, so it was quite obvious that they had established, secure jobs. That meant it was more like six safeties competing for two or three slots on the roster.

I truly felt like I carried the weight of the world on my back as I competed for a job on the West Coast. For starters, I was over 2,000 miles away from my wife and newborn daughter. Claire McKinley Pate was born June 29, 2001, in Opelika, Alabama; I was able to come home for the birth of our daugh-

Claire and Dana at Tiger Walk. *Courtesy of the author.*

ter and stay with my wife and baby girl for two weeks before training camp started. I can't even begin to describe to you what it is like to board a plane en route to the other side of the country for an unknown amount of time as your wife, with your newborn child, waves goodbye at the boarding gate. I cried, I was mad, I was lonely, and I felt selfish. I questioned my priorities and the strain I left on my wife. I take my hat off to our military's men and women who do this on a routine basis.

I was also bothered by the fact that one entire year remained of undergraduate work at Auburn. This was worrisome to me for this reason. If I were to be cut from the Chargers team after fall semester at Auburn had started, that would alter my plans of optometry school one whole year. If they cut me before or even a few weeks into that fall semester, I could finish my undergraduate work, apply to optometry school, and enter in the fall class of 2002. The absolute worst circumstances that could possibly happen would be for me to be dismissed from the Chargers in the middle of the semester, making me postpone optometry school until the fall of 2003.

I carried this anxiety and fretfulness with me through one week of training camp, when I finally decided to voice my concerns to my position coach, Rod Perry. I approached Coach Perry after a defensive backs meeting early one morning and told him that if I was going to be cut, to cut me early on in the trimming-down process. That way I could complete my undergraduate work at Auburn and apply to optometry school in that same year. Coach Perry looked at me, totally shocked, to put it extremely mildly. He reassured me that my hard work was not going unnoticed and that the defensive coordinator, Coach Joe Pascale, was pushing for and would likely get five roster slots for safeties instead of just four. By the end of that early-morning practice on the campus of the University of California at San Diego, the defensive coordinator as well as the head coach, Coach Mike Riley, approached me and told me I was doing great and I should just relax and continue to make plays when opportunities presented themselves.

Opportunities to make plays in an NFL practice when you're not a starter are few and far between. Whenever we performed full-team drills, we had basically two full teams rotating in four-play series. The starters went four plays, then the second team went four plays, and then back to the starters for four plays, etc. That was the method of rotation. That meant that the starters got half of all snaps in practice as everyone else rotated every other four-play series. So as I mentioned previously, we had eight safeties competing for four or five roster slots, meaning six of us were rotating onto the practice field every 20th play or so.

It's pretty tough to make an impression when your opportunities are limited and your biggest challenge, at least mine was, is your emotional psyche. You feel like you're just there to hold a dummy during a drill for a starter or to line up as a scout punt-block team against the starting punt team, and for all practical purposes, that's exactly why free agents are there. But in the back of your mind you know that a handful of rookie free agents make every team and that the bottom line is winning football games. Period. If you bring something to the table that might contribute to the success of a football team winning, then you've got a shot of making a roster even if it's ahead of an experienced veteran (after all, your services come at a much cheaper cost to the team). It is a daunting challenge to balance these two opposing thought processes on a daily basis.

About midway through training camp, I was plunged in a familiar role, that of being asked to learn both safety positions at the same time. I viewed this assignment presented to me by Coach Perry as an indication that I was making enormous strides and that I was doubling my value as backup (one guy who could back up two positions).

As each week passed, players came and went, yet I remained. Confidence began to build with each passing day as the 53-man roster was slowly but surely being created. By the time our final preseason game rolled around, there wasn't a whole lot of trimming down left to do as we took about 65 players to Phoenix, Arizona. Little did I know, this contest would be my last football game ever.

I entered the game for the first time to start the second quarter on a night when the temperature at kickoff was 101 degrees for an 8:00 p.m. start. To those who say the heat out West is no big deal and more tolerable because of the lack of humidity, I must laugh at you. Trying to play that game in Phoenix was like breathing the exhaust from an 18-wheeler. On the second series of the second quarter, I was playing man coverage on Arizona's slot receiver when they ran a stop/hitch route to him. I had an outstanding break on the ball and arrived just as the ball touched his hands and really put a big hit on the receiver, tackling him for no gain. It was probably my best play in a Chargers uniform, but it was the last play of my career. I dislocated my left shoulder in the process of that tackle, and less than 15 hours later, I was cut from the roster.

Without going into extreme detail, I'll just state that the manner in which the San Diego Chargers treated me after my injury was sincerely scandalous on the part of the Chargers organization, in particular their haughty front office. Thank God I had an agent who sought out his client's best interests and was up to date on injury rules and regulations and physicians back home in Alabama who recognized the extent of my injury and the proper time table for recovery.

I enjoyed my NFL experience, though, as short as it may have been and as mistreated as I may have felt because I proved to myself that I could play with the best athletes in the world. And the funny thing is had I made the roster and moved my family out to San Diego, I wouldn't be there now. Less than two years after I was let go, not a single safety who was on the squad when I left is still with the Chargers (one of them was an All-Pro performer and another is out of the league altogether). That's the business and the life in the National Football League. But as I opened this section saying, I firmly believe the NFL was not God's will for my life, and as I examine all of the various ways He tried to tell me just that, it's somewhat comical and somewhat embarrassing how I thought I could out-maneuver the King of Kings.

The Bowden Saga

Were players being paid while Terry Bowden was head coach at Auburn University? Well, apparently his answer to that question was yes, some players were being paid upon his arrival to Auburn, but no, he wasn't directly paying players—the boosters were doing the honors. An off-the-record interview in September 2003 unveiled that illegal payments were being made to a few players on the Auburn football team and that this pattern of payment extended from Coach Pat Dye's tenure and into Bowden's time as coach. Coach Bowden insisted that he put an end to the payments after a couple of years at the helm, which would have been when I was in high school. But he then neglected to report this infringement of NCAA rules and signed compliance reports that indicated that to his knowledge, there were no violations under his program.

I spent a good portion of my book somewhat defending Coach Bowden and the program he headed up and presented to us all. Did I fool-heartedly drink the Kool-Aid and just want to believe that the guy was committed to playing by the rules and running a clean, honorable program? From what I saw, heard, and experienced during my stint at Auburn, much to the chagrin of legions, he did just that; he was by the book. Of course there are those who had closer relationships to Coach Bowden than I ever did who may claim otherwise and may do so validly, but I can only comment from my own personal experiences from a player's perspective (which in most cases is from the outside looking in).

Do I think he was totally innocent and not at fault if his off-the-record interview is accurate? No way. If he knew players were getting paid upon his arrival to Auburn, should he have reported these findings to the NCAA? Probably. Would that have meant a without-question dismissal from his position as head coach at Auburn University? There's no doubt it would have. If he knew, yet chose to sit on the information, do I blame him? What was his alternative, risk being fired for reasons revolving around the decisions and actions during the previous administration's tenure? I don't know that I would have handled it much differently.

However, the interview was ridiculous and should have never occurred. If you've got something to hide, for your sake and for many others, hide it. You don't go exclaim it to a sports reporter of all people. And on top of that, you don't contort yourself to be the hero even if you truly were. You are the head coach, the CEO of the program. If the program falls, you're ultimately the man the finger points to.

But hey, what do I know? As this entire book hopefully demonstrated, the players are last to know anything and everything, and this instance is no different except, of course, for the players who were receiving improper benefits.

But that raises my next question, and it's a question posed to the boosters from every school in America: how do you decide which players to pay? I mean, do you pay only starters? Only black or white players? Only guys from your state? What exactly is the criteria for a player who deserves a little "extra?" It's obviously not based on need, because I've already discussed my financial situation while at Auburn. It's not starters, because I was one for four consecutive years. What is it, then, that makes a teammate so much more deserving of a gift of money than someone like me? Perhaps you were just certain I would have never accepted your money, which would have been a correct assumption, or maybe you thought I didn't need or deserve "booster financial aid." Whatever your reasons were, it sure does leave me wondering just how you target your pay-for-play players.

However, as a former player, alumnus, and now fan of Auburn, I'm proud that I can say that no one ever approached me concerning this issue, as surprising as that may be.

UAB School of Optometry

I can't begin to tell you how excited I am regarding my career choice. Optometry is truly a unique, unparalleled profession that offers on overabundance of positive, appealing aspects. The opportunity to care for people and to have the ability to restore, improve, and protect the most precious of all senses— the sense of sight—is a remarkably satisfying enterprise. The combination of medicine, fashion, business, and tremendous technological advances offers a realm of work that is challenging, uplifting, and beneficial to the community.

I am also lucky enough to be one of 40 individuals a year who are educated at the best school of optometry in the world. The UAB School of Optometry boasts a program complete with faculty, facilities, and in some instances, students who are unmatched by any other program.

Unfortunately for me, the year 2007 must come before I can practice.

Auburn Football:
The Current State of Affairs

"Embarrassing" and "reprehensible" come to mind when reflecting on the manner in which Auburn University conducted their unscrupulous quest for a new head football coach prior to the 2003 Iron Bowl. And unfortunately, in my opinion, this type of bungled, inept decision making with regard to football coaches at Auburn University has become the norm instead of an atypical anomaly. As much as I reviled and resented Coach Bowden's decision to quit on us in the middle of a despicable season in 1998, I firmly believed he deserved better treatment from Auburn University. When Auburn University promised Coach Oliver the head job only to retract this offer in place of Coach Tuberville, it was obvious to me, and many others, that Auburn treated Bill Oliver inappropriately. And the pattern continued when Coach Tuberville was humiliated by the attempt to lure University of Louisville coach Bobby Petrino to Auburn without even the decency of a courtesy call to the University of Louisville and then was left to ponder his future without the civility of even a congratulatory phone call following an Iron Bowl victory. Both Tommy Tuberville and Louisville deserved better treatment and proper respect from Auburn University.

Following this episode of fraudulent behavior by Auburn's leadership, Auburn received notice from SACS (Southern Association of Colleges and Schools) in December 2003 that it was being placed on probation for, among many other things, displaying lack of institutional control, specifically citing its athletics department. The organization seemed especially concerned with important decisions and financial control coming from a minority of members on the Board of Trustees, not the president of university. Auburn has one year to show countering evidence and to comply with the investigation.

Auburn's first step in satisfying SACS came with the resignation of William Walker from his position as president. What was likely to be perceived as a positive move in the eyes of SACS may have been neutralized by the Board's decision to promote from within Auburn's newest president, Dr. Ed Richardson. Will SACS officials find it difficult to understand the rationale of promoting a man from within the Board, even if his Board duties were by virtue of his previous job as state superintendent, when it is micromanagement by this very Board that SACS is seeking to eliminate? Let's hope not. However, it would not surprise me if they view this as a few Board members continuing their reign over the institution's affairs.

One of the first lessons you learn as a football player at Auburn is that no one player is bigger than the program. Many came before you, and many more will follow. You learn to accept the fact that Auburn will go on being Auburn with or without you. However, I believe the problem at Auburn University is that there are a select few in leadership roles as members of the Board of Trustees who believe they truly are bigger than Auburn University.

Now let me say this, I believe in Athletic Director David Housel. His love and admiration for Auburn radiates from him and should be questioned by no one. I believe he has moved Auburn athletics forward in virtually every sport, giving the coaches the essential elements they need to run successful programs. From a player's perspective, he was always accessible, friendly, and extremely gracious for the effort we put forth, and we appreciated someone who actually knew us by our first names. I believe David to be a tremendous ambassador for

Auburn and also believe he would have been an upper echelon athletics director if he were allowed to wield the power that other athletic directors are given. Instead, the Board of Trustees, especially Bobby Lowder, believe they should put on the athletic director hat whenever they see fit, thus reducing the power that David Housel should have.

I believe a better way to look at the power structure controlling Auburn athletics is this: Do you think Tommy Tuberville worries more about his relationship with David Housel or Bobby Lowder? You know the answer, and that's the problem with Auburn University—too many people are worried about their relationship with Bobby Lowder.

Now, I wouldn't know Bobby Lowder if he walked through my front door. In the time I spent at Auburn, I heard his name mentioned many times, yet his face eluded me throughout my entire playing days as a Tiger. He may be a remarkable person for all I know, and I really shouldn't condemn the man for all of Auburn's faults without knowing all of the details and circumstances surrounding why and how he acts on Auburn's behalf. But one detail is clearly evident to me, how can Bobby Lowder know the heart and needs of a football program, thus the direction that program needs to steer toward, if he never even takes the time to get to know its players. In my opinion he cannot, which is why the athletic director—the man with the title *Athletic Director*—should make decisions within the realm of sports and not a banker from Montgomery. I'm fairly confident David Housel doesn't advise Bobby Lowder on how to properly invest his money or how to appropriately run Colonial Bank. Bobby Lowder should return the favor and not counsel David Housel on how to run an athletics department.

To his credit, I believe most would agree Bobby Lowder's benevolence to give back to Auburn University is without comparison. I concede the fact the money and time Mr. Lowder has graciously given to Auburn has lead to further advancement in a variety of areas on campus. I would like to believe the man has Auburn's best interests at heart, and that his chief impediment is simply his unbridled passion for the school prompting him to act in the majority of school decisions. With that being said however, there are other Auburn visionaries who have been waiting in the wings for quite some time now to lead and exact successes for the university they adore. Will their opportunity ever arrive?

I must say I was saddened to see David Housel decide to "retire" effective January 2005. Though his actions in the Bobby Petrino–Louisville fiasco left a lot to be desired, I firmly believe the man was carrying out the will of his superiors. I believe that Auburn athletics, when taken as a whole and judged beyond just that of football, soared to new heights under David's watch, and he should receive praise for that. I believe 40 years of service to an institution is immeasurable; my only wish was that the man had been given the opportunity to run his department uninhibited. To the new athletic director, my advice to you would be this—find a good chiropractor—the force generated when those strings pull you from Montgomery will be severe.

With regard to Coach Tuberville, Auburn should be thankful and jubilant that Coach Tuberville decided to continue serving Auburn as its head football coach despite the dreadful treatment he received from Auburn officials. I know Coach Tuberville to be a good person and a superior coach, a coach that practically rebuilt a football program from scratch and has elevated expectations at Auburn to such enormous heights that it nearly cost the man his job.

Tuberville came to Auburn and inherited one of the worst Auburn football teams in the institution's long history. He

Attending an Auburn Tiger Walk for the first time as a fan with my friends. (Left to right) Jay and Barbara Sanders; Dana, Claire, and me; and Matt and Jill Mullinax. *Courtesy of the author.*

became heir to a program in disarray and to a group of players that wanted nothing to do with him or his assistant coaches, but somehow, he won us all over, he made us competitive, and he made us believe in ourselves again. If nothing else, Tommy Tuberville deserves high marks for breathing life back into Auburn football.

Only time will tell what the future holds for Auburn University. My hope is that Auburn men and women will take back their university and triumph over the inadequacies that exist in Auburn's administration and Board. I know Auburn to be a remarkable place and an outstanding institution, Auburn athletics to be among the nation's elite, and Auburn people to be unequaled. Because of this, Auburn will prevail over any obstacle hurled its way even when those obstacles come from within. War Eagle!

APPENDIX

Honors/Awards

Bryant-Jordan Scholarship Winner (1997)
Four-Year Starter on Football Team (1997-2000)
Freshman All-SEC Team (1997)
SEC Academic Honor Roll (1998-2001)
Coaches All-SEC Second Team (1998)
Preseason All-SEC Second Team (1999, 2000)
Four-Time Team Captain, voted by teammates (1999, 2000)
GTE/CoSIDA Academic All-American, All-District (1999, 2000)
National Football Foundation College Football Hall of Fame Award Recipient,
    Auburn Chapter (2000)
Pat Dye Leadership Award (2000)
Highest GPA on Football Team Award (2000)
United States Achievement Academy All-American Scholar (2000)
CW Streit Award, presented annually to the senior with the highest scholastic
    record (2000)

Career Defensive Statistics

Year	G/GS	TT	UT	AT	TFL-YDS	QBS-YDS	FF/FR	PD	INT
1997	13/8	50	31	19	0-0	0-0	0/0	8	0
1998	10/9	70	40	30	4-8	0-0	0/2	3	2
1999	11/11	59	39	20	5-17	2-6	0/0	4	3
2000	13/12	35	24	11	2-7	2-13	0/0	5	2
Total	47/40	214	134	80	11-32	4-19	0/2	20	7

G=Games
GS=Games Started
TT=Total Tackles
UT=Unassisted Tackles
AT=Assisted Tackles
TFL=Tackles For Loss

QBS=Quarterback Sacks
YDS=Yards
FF=Fumbles Forced
FR=Fumbles Recovered
PD=Passes Defended
INT=Interceptions

Celebrate the Heroes of College Football
in These Other 2004 Releases from Sports Publishing!

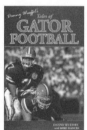
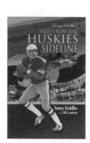

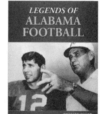